IBM® Microcomputer Assembly Language in 10 Programming Lessons

IBM® Microcomputer Assembly Language in 10 Programming Lessons

Julio Sanchez
Northern Montana College

Maria P. Canton
Skipanon Software Co.

PRENTICE HALL, Englewood Cliffs, New Jersey 07632

Library of Congress Cataloging-in-Publication Data

SANCHEZ, JULIO,

  IBM microcomputer assembly language in 10 programming lessons /
Julio Sanchez, Maria P. Canton.

    p.   cm.

  Includes bibliographical references and index.

  ISBN 0-13-726407-0

  1. IBM microcomputers—Programming. 2. Assembler language
(Computer program language) I. Canton, Maria P. II. Title.

QA76.8.I259193S27 1992   91-12423
005.265—dc20   CIP

Acquisitions editor: *Marcia Horton*
Production editor: *Jennifer Wenzel*
Cover designer: *Lundgren Graphics*
Copy editor: *Brenda Melissaratos*

Prepress buyer: *Linda Behrens*
Manufacturing buyer: *Dave Dickey*
Supplements editor: *Alice Dworkin*
Editorial assistant: *Diana Penha*

© 1992 by Prentice-Hall, Inc.
A Simon & Schuster Company
Englewood Cliffs, New Jersey 07632

The author and publisher of this book have used their best efforts in preparing this book. These efforts include the development, research, and testing of the theories and programs to determine their effectiveness. The author and publisher make no warranty of any kind, expressed or implied, with regard to these programs or the documentation contained in this book. The author and publisher shall not be liable in any event for incidental or consequential damages in connection with, or arising out of, the furnishing, performance, or use of these programs.

Printed in the United States of America

10 9 8 7 6 5 4 3 2 1

ISBN   0-13-726407-0

TRADEMARK INFORMATION

AT and XT are trademarks of International Business
  Machines Corporation.
BASIC is a registered trademark of the Trustees of
  Dartmouth College.
CP/M is a registered trademark of Digital Research
  Inc.
IBM, IBM PC/XT/AT and PC-DOS are registered
  trademarks of International Business Machines
  Corporation.
Intel is a registered trademark of Intel Corporation.
MS-DOS is a trademark of Microsoft Corporation.
Microsoft is a registered trademark of Microsoft
  Corporation.
UNIX is a registered trademark of AT&T
  (Bell Laboratories).

Prentice-Hall International (UK) Limited, *London*
Prentice-Hall of Australia Pty. Limited, *Sydney*
Prentice-Hall Canada Inc., *Toronto*
Prentice-Hall Hispanoamericana, S.A., *Mexico*
Prentice-Hall of India Private Limited, *New Delhi*
Prentice-Hall of Japan, Inc., *Tokyo*
Simon & Schuster Asia Pte. Ltd., *Singapore*
Editora Prentice-Hall do Brasil, Ltda., *Rio de Janeiro*

Contents

Contents **vii**

Preface

Assembly is the most intimidating of all programming languages. Those of us who learned the language some time ago and continue to use it regularly forget the fright and confusion that resulted from our first encounter with opcodes and operands, instructions and directives, binary and hexadecimal, ROM and RAM, and scores of other enigmatic words in the assembly language terminology. In this respect many textbooks provide little reassurance to the dismayed student. Assembly language authors (present company included) have often been more concerned with the exactitude and correctness of their statements than with their clarity and simplicity.

This book is an effort at reducing some of the inherent difficulty and the psychological consternation usually associated with a first course in assembly language programming. Our approach has been to make the information easier to assimilate by reducing its complexity. For example, we have used 31 of over 100 operation codes in the 8086 instruction set, and 7 of over 40 assembler directives. Certainly this simplification implies some loss in the rigor of the material presented and in the elegance of the code samples. For example, we have completely bypassed certain subjects, including the more complex 8086 addressing modes, mathematical programming, string instruction, stack manipulations, and other complications that are not strictly required at the elementary level. Because performance of any skill must be acquired gradually, we have felt free to limit our present aim to providing a first and unpretentious level of programming achievement.

On the other hand, we have stressed certain subjects and programming habits that we think should be emphasized from the start. Many students approach a programming project by turning on the computer and executing the editor program, not realizing that programming is not merely typing the code, but also designing, planning, thinking, and organizing. We have tried to stress this intellectual element by underlining the usefulness of flowcharts, which are introduced in the first chapter and used in illustrations and examples throughout the text.

The books are designed for use in a computer lab setting, in which each student has access to a machine or terminal. The ideal teaching environment includes a screen projector attached to the instructor's machine, but this piece of equipment is not strictly required. Each programming lesson contains a sample program that illustrates the functions, keywords, and language elements covered in the chapter. Except for some introductory material presented in the first session, each class meeting can be approached as a series of explanations and discussions of the corresponding lesson program. Additionally, the lesson programs serve the instructor as unobtrusive lecture notes. A vocabulary list, questions, and programming exercises are included in each chapter. The exercises have been designed at several levels of complexity, allowing for some individualization of the course contents, within its elementary nature.

The book is intended for students with little programming skills, although some typing ability and familiarity with the machine must be assumed. Our fundamental aim has been to provide a self-contained textbook for undergraduate-level courses often required in electronics, computer science, and computer information systems programs. We believe that the text is suited also for many courses offered by community colleges, vocational, and technical schools. Some advanced classes at the high-school level could also find it useful.

The text is compatible with all popular assembly language development systems for the IBM microcomputers, including Microsoft Macro Assembler (MASM), Microsoft Quick Assembler, Intel ASM-86, Borland Turbo Assembler, and others.

The authors would like express their appreciation to friends and associates who have provided help and support in this project. In particular, at Prentice Hall we would like to thank Marcia Horton, series editor, her assistant Diana Penha, and Jennifer Wenzel in the Production Department. At Northern Montana College we are grateful to Dr. Martha Ann Dow and Kevin Carlson.

Great Falls, Montana   *Julio Sanchez*
                                                                           Maria P. Canton

IBM® Microcomputer Assembly Language in 10 Programming Lessons

1

Programming Languages and Tools

1.0 WHAT IS ASSEMBLY LANGUAGE?

Most of us do not think of computers as devices similar to automobiles, sewing machines, or lawn mowers, yet computers are machines. In the United States the largest society of computer professionals is named the Association for Computing Machinery (ACM). The reason for this dissociation is that we often link the word "machine" with a device composed of mechanical moving parts in the form of gears, shafts, and levers. The computer is an electronic, digital device that performs its work not by turning gears and shifting levers but by the action of electrons in electrical circuits. All this notwithstanding, there are moving parts in most computers and many of today's conventional mechanical devices often contain electronic digital circuits.

Because computer are machines, the set of instructions used in communicating with computers is called *machine language*. Machine language is often referred to as a *low-level language* in contrast with other programming languages, such as BASIC, Pascal, and C, which are called *high-level languages*. However, high-level languages are sets of machine language super instructions because machine language is the only way for directly communicating with the computer hardware.

An *assembler* is a software tool that aids in the development of machine language programs. The assembler allows the programmer to use symbolic words, names, and conventional numbers as a computer language instead of using meaningless machine codes. The set of symbolic instructions recognized by the assembler program is called *assembly language*. The assembler generates machine language codes, which are the only ones recognized by the computer hardware. Although it is possible to write programs

1

directly in machine language, there is no advantage in doing it the hard way, because it is much easier to create machine language code by using assembly language.

Note that the computer itself is not programmable. When we say that a computer is programmed in machine language we are actually referring to the programming of the individual electronic and electromechanical components that form the computer. These components include a central processing unit (CPU), memory, and various other electromechanical devices. For example, the assembly language programmer of an IBM microcomputer deals mainly with the machine's central processing unit and the system's memory. But occasionally the programmer needs to control other support devices, such as the keyboard controller, the video controller, the interrupt controller, the disk or diskette controller, and the printer and serial port hardware.

Why Learn Assembly Language?

Learning assembly language has both educational and practical purposes. In order to write programs that control the central processing unit, store and retrieve memory information, or change the operation of other electronic devices, the assembly language programmer has to gain considerable knowledge about each of these elements. Therefore, a course in assembly language programming is also a course in the machine to which it refers.

At the same time, because machine instructions generated by the assembler offer the only direct communications with the computer hardware, assembly language programs have substantially better performance than programs in high-level languages. This means that a program coded in assembly language runs faster and takes up less memory than an equivalent one coded in BASIC, Pascal, C, or any other high-level language.

In addition, high-level languages are limited to the functions and operations considered necessary or convenient by the creators of the language. For instance, in the IBM microcomputers, the developers of the BASIC programming language considered it important to give the programmer the ability to display data at any position on the video screen, whereas the creators of the Pascal language considered it unnecessary. Consequently, although the BASIC programmer can control the display position, the Pascal programmer is limited to displaying data sequentially, in a manner that is reminiscent of an adding machine tape. On the other hand, there are no language restrictions to assembly language code. The assembly language programmer has total and unrestricted power over the machine hardware and can program it to perform any operation of which it is capable.

1.1 THE IBM MICROCOMPUTER

In 1981 IBM introduced the first member of its microcomputer family, named the Personal Computer, or PC. Since then many models of this machine have been developed and marketed. The PC XT, which included a fixed disk drive, was released in 1983. In 1985, IBM unveiled a more powerful Personal Computer, named the PC AT, and a home-market model named the PCjr. In 1987 the Personal Computer line was replaced with a new generation of machines called the Personal System/2 (PS/2) line. This new line includes the low-end models 25 and 30, the more advanced models 50, 55, and 60, and the high-end machines models 70 and 80. In 1990 IBM revived the idea of a home computer with a line of inexpensive desktops called the Personal System/1 and in 1991 introduced the high-end model 90 and model 95, which use the more powerful microprocessor and are equipped with a new graphics system.

In addition to IBM many other companies manufacture computers that use similar hardware components and software. These machines are often called IBM-compatible microcomputers. Companies that manufacture IBM-compatible microcomputers include Tandy Corporation (Radio Shack), Compaq, and Hewlett-Packard.

In spite of variations in the different models of the IBM microcomputers and compatible machines, there are certain features that have remained unchanged:

1. All IBM microcomputers use a central processing unit of the Intel iAPX 80x86 family. These chips include the 8088 CPU, used in the original PC; the 8086, used in some versions of the model 25 and 30, the 80286, used in the PC AT and some machines of the PS/2 line, the 80386, used in the model 70 and 80. The newest member of the Intel iAPX 80x86 family, the 486, is used in the IBM model 90 and model 95 as well as in some non-IBM machines. There is also an 486 upgrade option for some versions of the PS/2 model 70.

2. All IBM and the IBM-compatible microcomputers are furnished with a fundamental program named Basic Input/Output System (*BIOS*). The BIOS program, which gains control automatically when the power is turned on, checks memory, tests and initializes the hardware components, and hands control over to the disk operating system program (DOS). BIOS provides many programmer's services that are accessible to assembly language programs. We will use many of these services in the programming lessons. Although the BIOS program has been modified and updated in practically every new IBM machine, the fundamental services and storage locations have remained unchanged.

3. All IBM microcomputers are furnished with the Microsoft disk operating system (MS-DOS), developed by Microsoft Corporation. Four major versions and over a dozen sub-versions of MS-DOS have been introduced since 1981. However, Microsoft has maintained the operating system's fundamental structure and services.

Machine Description

Figure 1.1 shows the essential components of a typical IBM microcomputer system.

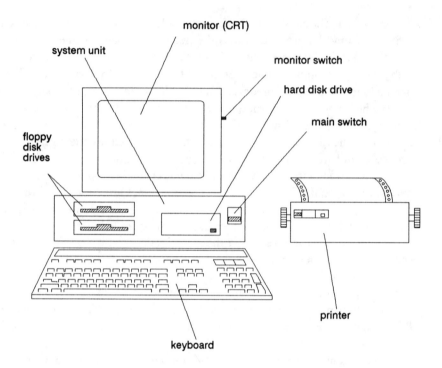

Fiigure 1.1   Principal Components of an IBM Microcomputer

System unit. The system unit is the enclosure that holds the fundamental elements of a computer system. In an IBM microcomputer the system unit contains a board of electronic components, sometimes called the *motherboard*. In the motherboard are the central processing unit, memory, the BIOS program chips, and the auxiliary controllers. Also in the system unit are connectors for expansion cards, a socket for an optional mathematical coprocessor chip, storage devices, such as floppy and fixed disk drives, and electronic ports for communicating with other devices.

Floppy disk drives. Floppy disks, or diskette drives, are removable electromagnetic devices used for storing computer data and programs. The diskette drive is often described as being similar to a record player turntable. The diskette holds data magnetically recorded on its surface, which is made of a special plastic called Mylar. The floppy disk has a central hole that engages in a drive mechanism. This mechanism makes the diskette spin on its axis while a read-write arm moves radially along the diskette's recorded surface.

All IBM microcomputers are equipped with at least one diskette drive. The older machines use a 5 1/4" diameter floppy disk. The newer machines use a 3 1/2" version of the floppy disk, which is encased in a plastic shell. The 3 1/2" model is usually called a microdisk. The capacity of a diskette drive is measured in the number of units of information (bytes) that can be stored in each diskette. The capacity of the floppy disk on IBM microcomputers has gone from 160,000 bytes in the original personal computer to over 1.4 million bytes in some of the newer models.

Fixed disk drive. The fixed disk drive is an electromagnetic device for storing data and programs; it is quite similar to the diskette drive previously described. Fixed disks are also called hard disks, or Winchester drives. The main difference between the diskette and the fixed disk system is that in the fixed disk the storage media is not removable from the drive. Hard disk drives usually contain several metal disks coated with a magnetic substance similar to the one used in the floppies. These metals disks are called *platters*.

Another difference between the floppy and the fixed disk drives is that the floppy drives spin the diskette only when data is being accessed, whereas the platters of a fixed drive start spinning when the computer is turned on. This determines that data can be accessed much more rapidly on a fixed disk because the fixed disk platters do not have to be brought up to speed before each read or write operation. In addition, fixed disk drives are built to a higher precision than floppy drives and are sealed from airborne particles that can damage the recording surface.

The capacity of a fixed disk drive is usually measured in megabytes of data that can be stored on its surface. One megabyte (1 Mb) is approximately equal to 1 million bytes. Popular fixed disk drive sizes in IBM microcomputers are 20, 40, 60, 80, and 120 megabytes.

The monitor. The computer monitor is a television-like screen used for displaying character data and graphic images. The monitor is part of the computer's video display system. It is sometimes called the CRT because its main component is technically named a cathode-ray tube. Because the monitor is used to transmit information to the user, it is considered an *output device*.

The keyboard. The keyboard is the device used to manually enter information and programs into the computer system. For this reason it is considered an *input device*. Most keyboards are connected to the system unit through a cable. One exception is the PCjr cordless keyboard, which communicates with the system using infrared waves.

The printer. The printer is a device for converting computer output into a permanent paper record. Although the printer is not a standard component of an IBM microcomputer, it is so useful that it is found in most systems. The technology used for producing the printed image can be by impact (dot matrix and daisy wheel) or by nonimpact methods (ink jet and laser). Printers and other devices that are not part of the standard system are sometimes called *peripherals*.

Starting the System

The start-up process for a computer system begins by the action of applying power to the system unit, the monitor, and other peripherals. Once power is applied in an IBM microcomputer, the system automatically executes the test programs that are part of the

BIOS. These routines, called the *power-on self-test* (POST), check that memory, central processing unit, and other essential controllers are in working order. If an error is detected, the process is immediately halted and a diagnostic message is displayed. If the system is found to be in working order, the BIOS reads the MS-DOS program from the diskette or hard disk and transfers execution to it. The process by which the computer tests itself and executes the operating system program is called the *bootstrap*.

MS-DOS, in turn, performs some additional hardware checks, initializes its devices and control areas, and configures the operating environment according to the user's instructions or to default values. What happens at this point depends on how each particular system is preset by the user. The following options are the most common:

1. MS-DOS displays a greeting message, optionally requests from the user the date and time of day, and awaits keyboard commands.

2. An application program is executed and given control automatically.

3. A graphical user interface (GUI) program gains control of the system and presents the user with a predefined set of selectable options.

In this book we will assume that some mode of option 1, above, is active as the system powers up. In other words, the user will have control of the system at what is called the DOS prompt. If your computer is preset to execute an application program (option 2) or a GUI (option 3), please refer to the corresponding documentation to determine how these options can be disabled or how execution can be directed to the DOS prompt.

Starting a fixed disk machine. IBM microcomputers equipped with a fixed disk are usually preconfigured so that MS-DOS will execute automatically on power-up. However, if a diskette is present in a floppy drive, the machine will attempt to read the DOS program off the diskette rather than the fixed disk. For this reason, except under special circumstances, the user of a system equipped with a fixed disk should make sure that the diskette drive or drives are empty before turning on the computer.

Starting a floppy disk machine. On the other hand, IBM microcomputers not equipped with a fixed disk require that an MS-DOS system diskette be present at start-up. Note that the diskette used for this purpose is not a data diskette, but one that contains the operating system software. The MS-DOS manual indicates which diskette provided with the system can be used for this purpose or how to prepare one.

IBM microcomputers are often equipped with more than one diskette drive. Under MS-DOS, diskette and fixed disk drives are designated with letters of the alphabet. The first and default diskette drive is designated as drive A. The system diskette must be placed in drive A at power-up. If there is a second floppy drive, it will be designated as drive B. The fixed disk drive is normally drive C, although it is possible to partition a hard disk drive into others designated with other letters. In this manner a system can appear to have disk drives C, D, E, F, and so forth.

Turning on the Switch. Because computer systems can be set up in many different ways and usually have several components, including peripherals such as a printer, the act of supplying power to it may vary. For example, the system in Figure 1.1 contains three independent power switches: one for the system unit, one for the monitor, and a third one for the printer. Note that the location of the power switches varies in different machines and models. To activate the system in Figure 1.1, the user has to turn on all three switches. Although the sequence in which these switches are activated is not critical, usual procedure is to start with the system unit, then the monitor, and last the switch on the printer.

In order to simplify the start-up operation, many computers are connected to a power strip or a multiple-line controller. These devices provide a single switch to supply power to several components. In this case the user will use the central switch instead of the individual switches located in each device or peripheral. However, the use of a power strip or similar device does not disable the individual switches on the devices and peripherals. If one of these individual switches has been intentionally or accidentally turned off, the central switch will not supply power to that device.

1.2 PROGRAMMING LOGIC

A set of logical instructions designed to perform a specific task is called a *program*. The document containing a set of instructions for starting a computer system could be described as a power-up program for a human operator. By the same token, a *computer program* is a set of logical instructions that will make the computer perform a certain and specific task. Note that in both cases the concept of a program requires a set of instructions that follow a logical pattern and a predictable result. A set of haphazard instructions that lead to no predictable end can hardly be considered a program.

The Flowchart

Programmers have devised logical aids that help them make certain that computer programs follow an invariable sequence of options and their associated actions. One of the most useful of these aids is called a *flowchart*. A flowchart is a graphical representation of the options and actions that form a program. Flowcharts use graphic symbols to enclose different types of program operations. Figure 1.2 shows the more common flowchart symbols.

The use of a flowchart is best illustrated with an example. Figure 1.3 is a flowchart of the program for turning on a computer system in which the components can be connected to the power line in three possible ways:

1. All computer components are directly connected to individual wall outlets.

2. All computer components are connected to a power strip and the power strip is connected to the wall outlet.

3. Some components are connected to a power strip, and some are connected directly to the wall outlets.

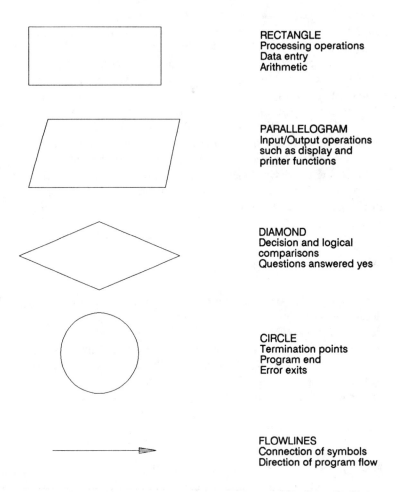

RECTANGLE
Processing operations
Data entry
Arithmetic

PARALLELOGRAM
Input/Output operations
such as display and
printer functions

DIAMOND
Decision and logical
comparisons
Questions answered yes

CIRCLE
Termination points
Program end
Error exits

FLOWLINES
Connection of symbols
Direction of program flow

Figure 1.2.   Flowchart Symbols

Note in the flowchart of Figure 1.3 that the diamond flowchart symbols are used to enclose program decisions. These decisions correspond to the principles of Aristotelian logic; therefore, there must be two and not more than two answers to the question. These possible answers are usually labeled YES and NO in the flowchart (see Figure 1.3). Decisions are the critical points in the program's logic. A program that requires no decisions or comparisons consists of such simple logic that a flowchart would be trivial and unnecessary. For instance, a flowchart that consists of three processing steps – start, solve problem, and end is logically meaningless.

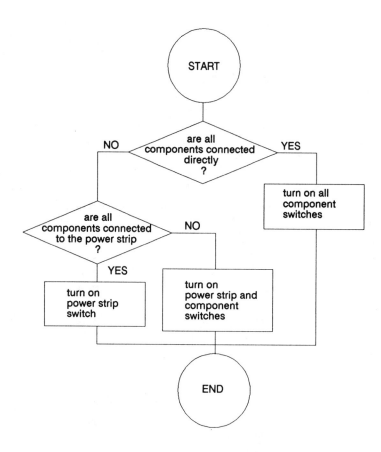

Figure 1.3 Start-up Flowchart

Computing machines of the present generation are not equipped with humanlike intelligence. Therefore, some assumptions that are obvious when dealing with human beings are invalid regarding computers. Computer programs can leave no loose ends and make no assumptions of reasonable behavior. You cannot tell a computer, "Well, you know what I mean." The programmer can use flowcharts to make certain that each processing step is actually specified.

1.3 MS-DOS

The standard operating system for the IBM microcomputers is MS-DOS. Four major versions of this program have been marketed since its original release in 1981. Each version is numbered with a single digit followed by a decimal point. The first MS-DOS version, released with the original Personal Computer, was designated version 1. This version, which had a short life span, was soon replaced with MS-DOS version 2.

Most IBM microcomputers in use today are equipped with MS-DOS version 3 or version 4. The releases or updates within an MS-DOS version are labeled with digits following the decimal point, for instance, MS-DOS version 3.1 and MS-DOS version 3.30. The second digit after the decimal point indicates a subrelease. IBM is also licensed to sell the MS-DOS operating system with its computers. These versions of MS-DOS are sold under the name PC-DOS. In spite of the several versions and updates, the most fundamental MS-DOS services and commands have remained compatible since version 2.0.

MS-DOS is a single-user, single-task operating system. This means that it is designed to be used in a single microcomputer and to run one program at a time. Other operating systems for the IBM microcomputers can run more than one program simultaneously; the best known one is Operating System/2 (OS/2). Other programs can operate in conjunction with MS-DOS to provide multitasking and a graphical interface. Two such programs are Microsoft Windows version 3.0 and DESQview/X.

MS-DOS provides two types of service: those intended for the conventional user and those intended for the programmer. MS-DOS programmers' services are directly available only from assembly language and are not normally accessible from the high-level languages. In this course we will cover several MS-DOS services. But a programmer must first learn to be a user of the system. Therefore, before we start writing programs we must be able to start the computer, to execute an application program, to access data and programs stored in the fixed disk or in diskettes, to prepare diskettes so that they can be used for storing data and programs, and to copy programs and data from one medium to another. In addition, as users and as programmers, it is convenient to have some fundamental understanding of the MS-DOS structures and conventions used in storing data and programs.

Executing a Program

Once the computer has been started and initialized (see "Starting the System" earlier in this chapter), we will see on the monitor a small flashing rectangle called the *cursor*. In MS-DOS the cursor is normally preceded by a greater than symbol (>) and the uppercase letter identifying the active disk or diskette drive. The screen message consisting of a drive letter, an optional directory name (explained later in this Chapter), the symbol, and the flashing cursor is sometimes called the *MS-DOS prompt*. This message indicates that MS-DOS is ready to receive a command.

The most used MS-DOS command is the one to execute a program stored in a fixed disk or diskette file. An interesting characteristic of this MS-DOS command is that it does not require a command word but simply the name of the program or file to be executed. In this manner, to execute the editor program named LED we type its name at the MS-DOS prompt and press the key labeled "Enter." In this book we will describe this action as follows:

```
LED <Enter>
```

Note that we have enclosed in angle brackets the letters that identify the key to be pressed. In this example, as soon as the key is pressed signaling the completed command, MS-DOS will search for an executable file named LED. If this file is found, the operating system will load it and transfer execution to the instructions that it contains. This operation is called *loading a program.*

Drives and Directories

In the IBM microcomputers, information is stored on magnetic diskettes or in a fixed disk. All machines have at least one disk or diskette drive, and most have two drives. The diskette drives are normally designated with the letters A and B. A fixed disk will appear as drive C, although it can be partitioned into more than one logical drive (D, E, F, and so on). Drives are designated by the drive letter followed by a colon, for example:

```
A:
```

Data stored in magnetic media are classified into directories and subdirectories. Every diskette or fixed disk drive contains a root directory, identified by the backslash (\). Directory and subdirectory names can have up to eight letters, numbers, and special symbols. The following symbols are allowed by MS-DOS in file and directory names:) , (# _ & $ % @ !.

The Pathname

The location of a file in the system's drive and directory structure is called the pathname. The pathname can contain a drive letter, one or more directories and subdirectories, and a filename. The following is an example of a pathname:

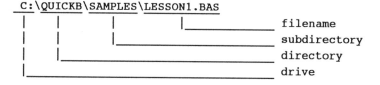

Not all pathnames have all of these elements. The following pathname contains only the drive and a filename:

```
A:\TEMPLATE.ASM
```

To *log on* to a drive type the drive letter followed by the colon symbol and press the <Enter> key. To log on to a directory or subdirectory type the command CD (change directory) followed by the backslash symbol and the pathname, for example:

```
COMMAND                  ACTION
C:                       log on to drive C
CD\QB                    log on to directory QB
```

Files and Filenames

An MS-DOS document or program is stored as a magnetic record called a file. MS-DOS files are identified by an eight-character filename and an optional three-character extension. The filename is separated by a period from the extension. Filenames can contain the letters and numbers as well as the symbols) , (# _ & $ % @ !. The following are MS-DOS filenames:

```
MYFILE_1.PRG
LEDC.EXE
```

The Directory Tree

The structure of directories and subdirectories in a diskette or fixed disk is called the directory tree. If no directories exist then the directory tree is simply the root directory. The MS-DOS TREE command displays the directory tree in the active drive. The following is a directory tree:

```
                DIRECTORY LEVEL
    root          level 1          level 2
     \            \DOS
                  \C_LANG          \INCLUDE
                                   \SYS
                                   \LIB
                  \QUICK_B
```

MS-DOS Wildcard Characters

MS-DOS allows the use of placeholder characters in filenames. The question mark (?) is a placeholder for any unspecified character. For example, the filename: LESSON?.BAS represents the following files:

```
LESSON1.BAS
LESSON2.BAS
LESSONA.BAS
```

The asterisk (*) is used to represent several unspecified characters in the filename or the extension fields. For example, the filename WP*.* represents the following files:

```
WP.EXE
WPDEMO.FIL
WPLISTA.DOC
```

whereas the filename LESSON1.* represents the files:

```
LESSON1.BAS
LESSON1.EXE
LESSON1.MAP
```

The filename *.* applies to all files whatever their filename or extension.

MS-DOS DIR Command

MS-DOS stores and maintains a list of all the files in each directory and subdirectory. Various forms of the MS-DOS DIR command can be used to examine the files and directories in a drive or the files and subdirectories in a directory. For example:

COMMAND	ACTION
DIR	Lists files in current drive, directory, or subdirectory
DIR A:	Lists files in drive A
DIR /P	Lists files and pauses after each full screen
DIR /W	Lists in compressed form
DIR \QB	Lists files in directory \QB
DIR *.ASM	Lists all files with extension .ASM
DIR *	Lists all files with no extension (can be used to list subdirectories)

Formatting

The MS-DOS FORMAT command checks a fixed disk, diskette, or microdisk for defects and creates a magnetic pattern of concentric circles that is necessary for storing data. WARNING: the FORMAT command erases all previously recorded data.

```
          IBM diskette and Microdisk Formats
CAPACITY         TYPE                SYSTEM
 360K           5 1/4" DD            PC, PC XT, and compatible
1200K           5 1/4" QD            PC AT, HP Vectra, and
                                     compatible
 720K           3 1/2" DD            PS/2 Model 25 and
                                     PS/2 Model 30
1440K           3 1/2" HD            PS/2 Model 30-386, 50, 70,
                                     80, 90, and compatible
```

To format a diskette or micro disk in drive A to the system's standard capacity type the command:

```
FORMAT A: <Enter>
```

To format a 360K diskette on a 1200K drive (AT or HP Vectra) type:

```
FORMAT A:/4 <Enter>
```

To format a 720K micro disk on a 1440K drive type the command:

```
FORMAT A:/N:9/T:80 <Enter>
```

To create a diskette or microdisk with the MS-DOS files required to start up the system (system disk), use the /S option of the FORMAT command, as follows:

```
FORMAT A: /S <Enter>
```

Copying Files

The MS-DOS COPY command is used to copy one or more files. The MS-DOS wildcard characters ? and * can be used with the copy command. For example, to copy all files from the root directory in drive A to the directory \QUICKB in drive C, type the command:

```
COPY A:\*.* C:\QUICKB <Enter>
```

To copy files from the current drive and directory, you may omit this parameter. For example, if you are logged on to drive A you may type:

```
COPY *.* C:\QUICKB <Enter>
```

Reproducing a Diskette or Microdisk

The MS-DOS DISKCOPY command is used to reproduce an entire diskette or microdisk for backup or other purposes. DISKCOPY automatically formats the destination medium if it has not been previously formatted or if the format is not compatible with the source. DISKCOPY cannot be used to copy groups of files. Use the COPY command and a global filename instead. To copy a microdisk or diskette in a single drive system type the command:

```
DISKCOPY A: B: <Enter>
```

In order to perform this operation MS-DOS creates a virtual drive B.

1.4 ASSEMBLY LANGUAGE PROGRAMMING TOOLS

In addition to the computer hardware, the assembly language programmer needs software tools. These software tools are nothing more than programs that help in the creation of other programs. Development packages for assembly language are available from several major software houses. The programs in this book were designed to be compatible with Microsoft's Macro Assembler (MASM). However, with minor modifications, the lesson programs listed in the book are compatible with any other assembly language development system.

The Editor

After a program is conceived, planned, flowcharted, and otherwise clearly defined, the next step in the development process is usually typing the program's instructions in a computer document. This document is called the *source file*. The software tool used in creating a program source file is called an *editor*.

Editors are designed for many specific purposes and come in many sizes and degrees of refinement. Word processors are complex editor programs devised for creating text documents such as letters, articles, and books. On the other extreme is the simple editor furnished with MS-DOS, named EDLIN, which is quite unsophisticated and therefore of limited use. Programming editors are a category of these text-creating programs specially suited for working with source files. Some assembly language development packages are furnished with more or less refined programming editors, whereas others do not include this software tool. In summary, the assembly language source file is usually created using one of the following editor options:

    1. The EDLIN editor furnished with all versions of MS-DOS. The instructions for using EDLIN are part of the MS-DOS documentation.

    2. A word processing program such as Wordperfect, Microsoft Word, or Wordstar. If a word processor is used as an assembly language editor, the source file must be saved so that it will not contain special word processor characters and control code that are not recognized by the assembler. Most word processing programs are equipped with an option (usually called the ASCII mode) that will strip these special characters from the user's file.

    3. A programming editor furnished with the development package, with another programming language, or purchased independently.

    One part of the programming task is the mechanical operation of typing source lines using an editor program. Whatever editor is chosen for this purpose, it is important to acquire some familiarity with its operation and commands before starting to learn and practice assembly language programming. The student should have also minimum typing skills. It is indeed a difficult task to learn assembly language while having to search the keyboard for each key to be pressed and trying to remember the operation and commands of an unfamiliar editor.

The Assembler

The assembler program is the most important element in the assembly language development system. Once the source file has been created and stored in a diskette or fixed disk (in a form that does not contain special characters or control codes) it is ready for assembly. Some programming packages allow invoking the assembler from within the editor. Perhaps a more common option is to exit the editor and invoke the assembler from the MS-DOS command line.

    The assembler program examines the instruction lines contained in the source file and generates a machine language encoding called the *object file*. If the assembler detects an error or inconsistency in the source, it will inform the programmer of the type of error encountered and of its location in the file. In this case the object file may or may not be generated depending on the mode of operation of the specific assembler and on the severity of the errors encountered.

The Linker

The object file generated by the assembler is an intermediate product. Although it contains the machine codes that can execute in the microprocessor, some important parameters are missing at this stage. The linker program is the step that usually follows assembly in the process of creating an executable program. In many cases linking is also the last step in this process.

The linker operates on the object files generated by the assembler. The purpose of the linker is to fill in the data that were not provided by the assembler, usually because these data are not available at assembly time. Linking is related to the computer environment. For this reason the linker is associated with the operating system and, in some cases, is furnished as part of the operating system software.

The name "linker" is related to the fact that several object files can be combined into a single executable file. In the IBM microcomputer system the executable files generated by the linker have the extension .EXE. These executable files (programs) are not restricted to specific memory areas but can be located anywhere in the user's memory space at load time.

Debuggers

Just as death and taxes are said to be unavoidable certainties in our lives, bugs are often considered the unavoidable certainty of computer programs. Assembly language programs, in particular, are usually judged to be more error prone than the high-level language counterparts. This is so because assembly language is more atomized; in other words, it takes more instructions to perform the same task. The more instructions in the code, the greater the possibility of an error.

A debugger is a software tool that allows, among other things, the controlled execution of another program. A program suspected of having an error can be executed by the debugger one assembly language line at a time, while the effect of each instruction is observed in the machine hardware. This action can be compared to a series of slow-motion X-rays revealing every detail of program execution. Although the process of actually locating the offending bug is often slow and laborious, in assembly language code there are no unknown elements in the software chain.

Like editors, debuggers are sometimes provided with the operating system software, with the development package, or purchased separately. To the student of assembly language a debugger program can also be a learning tool. By executing programs one instruction at a time (an operation called *tracing the code*) it is possible to actually observe the action of each instruction on the machine hardware. Note that this direct examination of a program's action is possible only in assembly language.

Other Development Tools

Assembly language development packages usually include other programs and utilities that serve specific purposes in the system; for instance, programs that are used in creating certain types of executable files, utilities that aid in managing programmer's files, and others used in performing specific conversions and file modifications.

VOCABULARY

assembler	keyboard
assembly language	linker
BIOS	machine lanhuage
bootstrap	memory
central processing unit (CPU)	monitor
debugger	motherboard
directory	MS-DOS
DOS prompt	object file
editor	output
execute	pathname
filename	peripherals
fixed disk drive	platter
floppy disk drive	POST
flowchart	program
hardware	software
high-level language	source file
input	system unit

QUESTIONS

1. What is the difference between low- and high-level languages?
2. Describe the function of an assembler.
3. List two advantages of assembly language compared to high-level languages.
4. Give the name of an output and of an imput device.
5. What is the BIOS POST?
6. What is the purpose of a diamond-shaped flowchart symbol?
7. What is the purpose of a circle-shaped flowchart symbol?
8. List the three elements that can be found in a pathname.
9. Explain the use of the MS-DOS * (asterisk) wildcard character.
10. Explain the purpose of the MS-DOS format command.
11. Give the name of the MS-DOS command use to reproduce a diskette or microdisk.
12. Explain the use of a linker program.

EXERCISES

1. Write a flowchart indicating the the sequence of steps necessary for starting your specific computer system.

2. Draw a map showing the drives and directory trees (if any) that are active in your system.
3. Format a system diskette and use it to start up your machine.
4. Create the following directory tree in the system diskette that resulted from exercise number 3:

```
DIR1 |  SUBDIR1A
     |  SUBDIR1B
     |  SUBDIR1C
     |
DIR2 |  SUBDIR2A
```

5. Copy two files from your fixed disk or from another diskette into the subdirectory SUBDIR1B of the diskette created in exercise number 4.

2

The Source File: Instructions and Directives

2.0 WHAT IS IN A SOURCE FILE STATEMENT

A *source file* is a document that contains the text of a computer program. In the present book the programs are coded in 80x86 assembly language. The name "source file" usually implies that the text is stored magnetically on a diskette or fixed disk. A printed version of the source file is usually called a *source file listing*. The source file is created using an editor program (see Chapter 1).

In the IBM microcomputer assembly language, source files are usually identified by a distinctive filename extension. In Microsoft's Macro Assembler system assembly language source files have the extension .ASM, whereas Intel's ASM 86 system uses the extension .SRC. Because the present book is designed to be compatible with the Microsoft assembler software, we will use the source file extension .ASM in our programs. At the end of this chapter you will find a listing of the source file named LESSON2.ASM.

An assembly language source file consists of a series of individual program lines called *statements*. In Figure 2.1 we show the structure and the component elements of an assembly language statement.

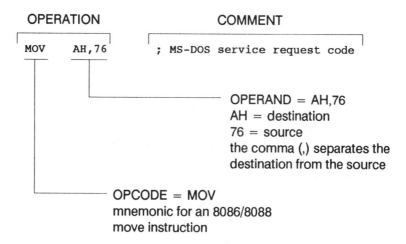

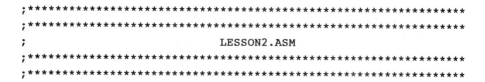

Figure 2.1 Parts of an Assembly Language Statement

Note in Figure 2.1 that the statement is divided into two fields, labeled operation and comment. The operation field of the source statement performs a processing function. The comment field usually contains some form of explanation of the statement.

The Comments Field

The semicolon (;) is used to separate the instruction from the comments field. Any text that follows the semicolon, up to the end of the line, is ignored by the assembler. Note in the listing of the program LESSON2.ASM, at the end of this chapter, that some program lines consist entirely of a comment. For example, the first five program lines in LESSON2.ASM are comments:

```
;**********************************************************************
;**********************************************************************
;                              LESSON2.ASM
;**********************************************************************
;**********************************************************************
```

On the other hand, in other program statements, such as the one in Figure 2.1, the comment field takes up only part of the line. Whether the comment field takes up the entire line or part of it, it is provided by the programmer for the benefit of any person trying to follow or interpret the code. Often the principal beneficiary of the comments is the programmer who wrote them. It is surprising how rapidly we forget the train of thoughts that led to a sequence of program operations. A program profusely commented will let us recall these thoughts so that we can remember our original logic. A badly or

uncommented program often is as undecipherable as a hieroglyphic. The following is a
version of the LESSON2.ASM program in which all the comment fields have been
removed.

```
STACK     SEGMENT stack
          DB       1024 DUP
STACK     ENDS
DATA      SEGMENT
GREETING DB        'Hello, I am your IBM computer$'
DATA      ENDS
CODE      SEGMENT
          ASSUME  CS:CODE
ENTRY_POINT:
          MOV     AX,DATA
          MOV     DS,AX
          ASSUME  DS:DATA
          LEA     DX,GREETING
          MOV     AH,9
          INT     21H
          MOV     AH,76
          MOV     AL,0
          INT     21H
CODE      ENDS
END       ENTRY_POINT
```

You may have noticed in the listing of the program LESSON2.ASM that comment
lines can be used to embellish the code and to highlight comments or critical points in
the program's execution. For example, three comment lines can be used to create a
graphical banner, as follows:

```
;*******************|
;   initialization  |
;*******************|
```

How much of this type of embellishment is used in the source is a matter of personal
preference. Each assembly language programmer eventually develops a personal style
that may or may not include the graphical use of comment lines.
Other program data are also often entered as comments in the source file. This
information can include the programmer's name, a copyright notice, the start and end
dates for the programming project, the date and contents of various updates and
modifications, or any other information that should be logged for future reference (see
text reference # 1 in LESSON2.ASM).

2.1 OPERATIONS

The "meat" of an assembly language source statement is the operation field. In 80x86 assembly language the operation field can contain a *microprocessor instruction* or an *assembler directive*. The operation field is the one used by the assembler in generating the machine codes.

Instructions

In the context of this book an instruction is a single operation of the 80x86 microprocessor. Note that although there are several programmable electronic and electromechanical components in an IBM microcomputer, the only one that can be directly accessed by the programmer is the 80x86 central processing unit. This means that the program must go through the CPU to access such devices as the video controller, the keyboard controller, or the disk controller. There are over 100 instructions in the 80x86 microprocessor. A great part of the task of learning assembly language is becoming familiar with these instructions.

The opcode. Each instruction is represented in assembly language with a mnemonic word called the *operation code,* or *opcode*. The letters that form the opcodes are chosen so that they remind us of the operation that they represent; for example, the opcode MOV represents a move operation, the opcode INC represents increment, and the opcode DIV indicates an arithmetic division. 80x86 opcodes contain from two to five letters, which can be entered in uppercase or lowercase letters or in both. In the listings of this book we have used uppercase letters for the opcodes so that they will stand out in the source, but other authors prefer lowercase letters.

The operand. In addition to the opcode, some 80x86 instructions contain a field called the *operand*. Whereas the opcode indicates an action to be performed by the instruction (verb element), the operand encodes the target, and sometimes the contents, of the action (noun element). In 80x86 assembly language operands can specify a CPU component (which can be either a *register* or a *port*), a location in the system's memory, or an immediate value. For example, the operand of the instruction in Figure 2.1

```
MOV     AH,76              ; MS-DOS service request code
```

specifies a register in the 80x86 CPU named AH and the immediate value 76. Once the instruction executes, the value 76 will be loaded (moved) into register AH. This instruction is used in the LESSON2.ASM program (see text reference # 2).

Although all 80x86 instructions must have an operation code, not all instructions have an explicit operand, because some 80x86 instructions perform such concrete operations that they do not require a distinct specification. For example, the instruction AAA (ASCII Adjust for Addition) is used in certain forms of 80x86 addition to modify the contents of the AL register. Because the action of the AAA instruction always takes place on the contents of the AL register, it does not require an operand.

In Figure 2.1 we observe that a comma (,) divides the operand into two fields. The comma, as used in an instruction operand, is sometimes called a *delimiter*. The field to the left of the comma is called the destination. The destination holds the target of the action performed by the instruction. The field to the right of the comma is called the source; it holds the origin or the contents of this action. In the instruction in Figure 2.1 the destination of the MOV (move) instruction is the processor's AH register, and the source (that which is moved) is the value 76.

But not all 80x86 operands have a distinct source and destination field. Some instructions perform actions in which the source is implicit or which do not require a source. For example, the instruction INC (increment) adds the value 1 to the operand. Because this added value cannot be changed, a source field is not required. Therefore the instruction to increment the AL register is coded as follows:

```
INC       AL                    ; AL = AL + 1
```

Addressing modes. The various ways in which an operand can be identified are called the *addressing modes*. For example, a memory location can be identified using its sequential number (direct addressing) or by a register that contains this value (register indirect addressing). Addressing modes are discussed in Chapter 4.

Assembler Directives

We have mentioned that the operation field of an assembly language statement can contain a microprocessor instruction or an assembler directive. Assembler directives are instructions to the assembler program. Notice that an instruction is an operational command to a hardware element of the system, whereas an assembler directive is a command to a software element. Instructions are determined by the characteristics of the microprocessor, whereas directives often change in different assembler programs. The following statement, taken from LESSON2.ASM (see text reference # 3) contains the DB (define bytes) assembler directive:

```
GREETING        DB       'Hello, I am your IBM computer$'
```

The word GREETING in this assembly language statement is a variable name. Variable names are invented by the programmer, usually so that the name represents the contents of the variable. The variable named GREETING in the above source line could have also been named HELLO_USER, FIRST_MESSAGE, or M1.

Assembler programs recognize dozens of directives. If learning the 80x86 instructions is the most important task for the assembly language student, then learning the assembler directives is the second most important one. Fortunately for the programmer, most commercial assemblers for the 80x86 are based on the original Intel assembler and use an almost identical set of assembler directives. This means that source files can be transported to other development systems with, at worst, minor modifications. But this is true only about the fundamental directives. Assembler programs often provide an extended set of directives that are particular to the program and will not be recognized by other assemblers. To avoid compatibility problems it is usually a good idea to avoid the use of nonstandard directives.

Labels

Labels are place markers in an assembly language program. Like variable names, labels are used by the assembler to define a position in the program. A difference between variable names and labels is that variable names are used to identify data items, whereas labels are used to mark places in the program's code. Another difference is that labels must end in a colon symbol (see text reference # 4 in LESSON2.ASM), whereas variable names do not. In the following code fragment the statement DOS_EXIT: is a label.

```
;******************|
;    exit to DOS   |
;******************|
DOS_EXIT:
        MOV     AH,76           ; MS-DOS service request code
        MOV     AL,0            ; No error code returned
        INT     21H             ; TO DOS
```

Identifiers

Variable names and labels are both considered *identifiers*. The syntax requirements for identifiers change in the different assembler programs. However, the following general identifier characteristics are valid in most commercial assemblers:

1. An identifier can contain letters and numbers, but the first character in an identifier must be a letter or a symbol.

2. Lowercase letters are converted to uppercase by the assembler; therefore, the names "GREETING" and "Greeting" appear to the assembler as the same variable.

3. Some symbols are also allowed in identifiers. Microsoft's Macro Assembler, for example, allows over 30 symbols. To maintain compatibility with other assemblers it is better to limit the use of symbols to the following special characters:

$$?, \quad \_, \quad \text{and} \quad @$$

4. Spaces are illegal characters because the assembler uses a space to detect the end of an identifier.

5. The maximum length allowed for an identifier depends on the specific assembler, but a limit of 30 characters will ensure compatibility with most systems.

2.2 THE STRUCTURE OF A PROGRAM

If we carefully look through the source listing of the LESSON2.ASM program, we will be able to distinguish three distinct program areas, as follows:

```
First area:
STACK    SEGMENT stack
            .
            .
STACK    ENDS

Second area:
DATA     SEGMENT
            .
            .
DATA     ENDS

Third area:
CODE     SEGMENT
            .
            .
CODE     ENDS
```

These areas are associated with the memory structure of the 80x86 microprocessors. The word "segment" used in all three areas is related to *segmented memory*, which is a characteristic of 80x86 systems. In Chapter 4 we discuss segments and segmented memory in detail. For the moment the following information will allow us use these areas in our programs, even though we may still not fully understand their structure and purpose. Note that the areas are discussed in a different order from the one in which they appear in the source.

The Data Area

The data area of and 80x86 assembly language program is devoted to storing program information. Here, the programmer places numeric variables and constants, text messages, and character strings, and reserves space for data generated by the user or by the program's own processing. Assembler programs provide a variety of directives and addressing modes that allow creating various types and sizes of data items. In the program LESSON2.ASM we have used the DB assembler directive to create a message string in the program's data area (see text reference # 3).

The Code Area

The program's code area contains program statements for the instructions to be executed by the microprocessor, as well as labels and comments. In other words, the code area holds the operations that are performed by the program.

The Stack Area

In 80x86 systems the stack area is an auxiliary data structure located in a reserved portion of the system's memory. The stack can be visualized as similar to the coin dispensers often used by bus drivers to store and disburse coins. In these spring-loaded coin dispensers, change is put in the device through the same slot through which the coins come out. Therefore, the last coin to be inserted is the first one to be discharged. In computer terminology this mode of operation is said to be *last in, first out* (LIFO).

A stack is a last-in-first-out structure used for the temporary storage of memory addresses and data items. An interesting feature of the stack area is that it is set up by the programmer but it is also used by the microprocessor and by the system software. Not all programs have their own stack. Later in this course we will meet a type of program that does not (in fact, cannot) have a stack. The program LESSON2.ASM, listed at the end of the chapter, does have its own stack (see text reference # 5). Notice that the DB assembler directive is used in the stack area as follows:

```
DB      1024 DUP ('?')   ; Default stack is 1K
```

This use of the DB directive differs from the one we saw in the data area. In the stack area the word DUP (duplicate) instructs the assembler to reproduce 1024 times the character enclosed in parenthesis. In memory measurements the value 1024 corresponds with 1 kilobyte (1K). The effect of the statement is to create a 1K stack area, initially filled with the ? symbol.

Using a Programming Template

If the stack area is defined exactly as in the program LESSON2.ASM, the Microsoft assembler will automatically create and initialize it for the programmer. In addition, LESSON2.ASM performs other preliminary operations that are usually necessary in creating an assembly language program. The resulting skeleton, composed of the areas named stack, data, and code, can be standardized so that the programmer need not reenter these statements with every source file. The following source file, named TEM-PLATE.ASM, performs this function:

```
;****************************************************************
;****************************************************************
;                        TEMPLATE.ASM
;****************************************************************
;****************************************************************
; Program title:
; Created by:
; Start date:
; Last modification:
;
; Program description:
;
;****************************************************************
;                        stack segment
;****************************************************************
STACK   SEGMENT stack
        DB      1024 DUP ('?')  ; Default stack is 1K
STACK   ENDS
;****************************************************************
;                        data segment
;****************************************************************
DATA    SEGMENT
;
DATA    ENDS
;****************************************************************
;                        code segment
;****************************************************************
CODE    SEGMENT
        ASSUME  CS:CODE
;******************|
;  initialization  |
;******************|
ENTRY_POINT:
; Initialize the DATA segment so that the program can access the
; stored data items using the DS segment register
        MOV     AX,DATA         ; Address of DATA to AX
        MOV     DS,AX           ; and to DS
        ASSUME  DS:DATA         ; Assume directive so that
                                ; the assemble defaults to DS
;********************************|
;            program code        |
;********************************|
```

```
;*******************|
;   exit to DOS     |
;*******************|
DOS_EXIT:
        MOV     AH,76           ; MS-DOS service request code
        MOV     AL,0            ; No error code returned
        INT     21H             ; TO DOS
;
CODE    ENDS
        END     ENTRY_POINT     ; Reference to label at which
                                ; execution starts
```

The student can copy the listing TEMPLATE.ASM to a disk or diskette file. To create a new assembly language program, a copy of the file TEMPLATE.ASM file can be loaded into the editor and renamed. This provides a fundamental programming framework that will save a substantial amount of effort.

2.3 BIOS AND MS-DOS PROGRAMMER'S SERVICES

We mentioned in Chapter 1 that the system software of an IBM microcomputer (BIOS and MS-DOS programs) provides various services for the benefit of programmers. These services, which are directly accessible by assembly language code, simplify the programming task by performing scores of frequently needed operations and functions. Appendices A and B of this book briefly describe some frequently used BIOS and MS-DOS programmer services.

Using an MS-DOS Service

The program LESSON2.ASM uses two MS-DOS programmer services (see text references #6 and #7). The first one is MS-DOS service number 9 of interrupt 21H, which is used to display a message string that ends in the $ sign. This MS-DOS service requires that the program using it set up a *pointer* to the data item that holds the message to be displayed. In assembly language terminology a pointer is a microprocessor register that holds the address of a data item. The 80x86 instruction LEA (load effective address) can be used to initialize a pointer register to a variable name, as in the following statement taken from the program LESSON2.ASM:

```
        LEA     DX,GREETING     ; Set DX to point to the start
                                ; of the item named GREETING
```

In addition to initializing a pointer to the message that is to be displayed, the program must also inform MS-DOS which programmer service is being requested. This is accomplished by the following statement in LESSON2.ASM:

```
MOV     AH,9            ; Load AH with the service
                        ; request number
```

Finally, the program must access the MS-DOS programmer services. In the IBM microcomputers MS-DOS programmer services are accessed through a mechanism called a *software interrupt*. The following statement in LESSON2.ASM is used to gain admission to the MS-DOS services:

```
INT     21H             ; Transfer control to MS DOS
                        ; interrupt 21H
```

The 80x86 microprocessors have available a total of 256 interrupts. In the IBM microcomputers some of these interrupts are used by hardware components, some are used by software routines (such as the MS-DOS programmer services just described), some are reserved for future functions, and some are left unused.

Several interrupts are devoted to the MS-DOS services; the most useful of these is interrupt 21H. In more recent versions of MS-DOS there are close to 100 programmer services available under this interrupt. Appendix B describes some of the most useful services of MS-DOS interrupt 21H. Note that the letter H in the term 21H represents a number in hexadecimal notation. Hexadecimal notation is a convenient system of numbers that is often used in computer technology. These and other number systems used in computer work are discussed in Chapter 3.

2.4 SOURCE CODE LISTING OF THE PROGRAM LESSON2.ASM

```
;****************************************************************
;****************************************************************
;                         LESSON2.ASM
;****************************************************************
;****************************************************************
;                                        |*******************|
;                                        | text reference # 1 |
;                                        |*******************|
; Program title: LESSON2
; Start date:
; Last modification:
;
```

```
; Program description:
; Display a screen message
;
; Program operations:
; 1. Initialize data segment
; 2. Display a message using DOS service number 9, INT 21H
; 3. Return control to DOS using service number 76, INT 21H
;
;****************************************************************
;                         stack segment
;****************************************************************
;                                        |********************|
;                                        | text reference # 5 |
;                                        |********************|
STACK    SEGMENT stack
;
         DB      1024 DUP ('?')  ; Default stack is 1K
;
STACK    ENDS
;
;****************************************************************
;                         data segment
;****************************************************************
DATA     SEGMENT
;                                        |********************|
;                                        | text reference # 3 |
;                                        |********************|
GREETING         DB      'Hello, I am your IBM computer$'
;
DATA     ENDS
;
;****************************************************************
;                         code segment
;****************************************************************
CODE     SEGMENT
         ASSUME  CS:CODE
;******************|
;  initialization  |
;******************|
;                                        |********************|
;                                        | text reference # 4 |
;                                        |********************|
```

```
ENTRY_POINT:
; Initialize the DS register so that the program can access the
; data items in this segment
        MOV     AX,DATA         ; Address of DATA to AX
        MOV     DS,AX           ; and to DS
        ASSUME  DS:DATA         ; Assume directive so that
                                ; the assemble defaults to DS
;
;*********************************|
;          program code          |
;*********************************|
;                                    |********************|
;                                    | text reference # 6 |
;                                    |********************|
; Display a message stored in the data segment using DOS service
; number 9, INT 21H. The message must end in a $ sign
        LEA     DX,GREETING     ; Set DX to point to the start
                                ; of the item named GREETING
        MOV     AH,9            ; Load AH with the service
                                ; request number
        INT     21H             ; Transfer control to MS DOS
                                ; interrupt 21H
;******************|
;   exit to DOS    |
;******************|
;                                    |********************|
;                                    | text reference # 7 |
;                                    |********************|
; After the message is displayed the program gives control back
; to MS-DOS using service number 76
DOS_EXIT:
;                                    |********************|
;                                    | text reference # 2 |
;                                    |********************|
        MOV     AH,76           ; MS-DOS service request code
        MOV     AL,0            ; No error code returned
        INT     21H             ; To MS-DOS
;
CODE    ENDS
        END     ENTRY_POINT     ; Reference to label at which
                                ; execution starts
```

VOCABULARY

addressing modes   opcode
assembler directive   operand
code area   segmented memory
data area   software interrupt
delimiter   source file
label   stack area
LIFO   statement
microprocessor instruction   variable name

QUESTIONS

1. What is a source file?
2. What symbol is used to mark the start of a program comment?
3. How does the assembler use the instruction's operation field?
4. What is another name for the operation code?
5. What are the two parts of the operand field?
6. What symbol is used to separate the source from the destination operand?
7. Is it possible to have an instruction with no explicit operand?
8. What is the difference between an instruction and an assembler directive?
9. What symbol is used to mark the end of a label?
10. How can you tell the difference between a variable name and a program label?
11. Can a space be embedded in an identifier?
12. List two program elements commonly placed in the data segment.
13. What do we mean when we say that the stack is a LIFO structure?

EXERCISES

1. Assemble, link, and run the program LESSON2.ASM using your own software development tools.
2. Modify the program LESSON2.ASM so that the message displayed includes your name.
3. Edit the program LESSON2.ASM and change one variable name and two labels.
4. Use Appendix C to locate the assembler directives in the program LESSON2.ASM. Make a list of the segments and segment names in the program.

3

Number Systems and the Microprocessor

3.0 NUMBER SYSTEMS FOR COMPUTER WORK

Numbers are a cultural product, but one number system, called the decimal system, has gained almost universal acceptance. The symbols used in the decimal system are the Hindu-Arabic numerals. We are so familiar with the symbols of the decimal system (0, 1, 2, 3, 4, 5, 6, 7, 8, and 9) that we tend to consider them a natural phenomena, although, in reality, any system of numbers is an intellectual convention. It if often said that the decimal system of numbers resulted from the practice of counting with our fingers and that if humans had 6 fingers instead of 10 our number system would have 6 symbols instead of 10.

This leads us to the fact that the fundamental use of a system of numbers is counting. The simplest form of counting is by tallying. The tally system, to which we all occasionally resort, consists of drawing a vertical line to correspond with each counted element. A refinement of the tally system is to make groups of five elements by drawing a diagonal line for each fifth unit counted, as follows:

$$ \text{LHt} \quad \text{LHt} \quad \text{LHt} \quad \text{II} $$

The tally system does not require numerical symbols. Roman numerals probably derived from the tally system because we can detect in some Roman numerals the vertical and diagonal traces used in tallying. For example, in the early version of the Roman numerals the numbers from one to five were represented as follows:

```
I, II, III, IIII, V
```

The uncertainty in the positional value of the digits, the absence of a symbol for zero, and the fact that some digits required more than one symbol, complicate the rules of arithmetic using Roman numerals.

The Hindu-Arabic numerals were introduced into Europe during the 14th and 15th centuries. These numerals are used in a counting scheme where the value of each digit is determined by its column position (decimal positional system), as in this example:

```
7 9 6 2
| | | |_____  units
| | |_____  10 units
| |_____  100 units
|_____  1000 units
```

The total value is obtained by adding the column weights of each unit

```
      7000 ——– 7 thousand units
       900 ——– 9 hundred units
+       60 ——– 6 ten units
         2 ——– 2 units
      ____
      7962
```

Binary Numbers

The computers built in the United States during the early 1940s, used decimal numbers and analog electrical circuits. In 1946 John Von Neumann and others decided that the computing machinery was easier to build and performed more reliably if the electronic circuits were based on two states, using cells that were either on or off. Because mathematicians had discovered that it is possible to count and perform arithmetic operations using a set of numbers consisting only of two symbols, the two states of an electronic cell could be made to correspond with the binary digits 0 and 1, thus creating a simple, calculating machine. This match explains the enduring relation between digital electronics and the binary system of numbers.

The binary system of numbers is the simplest possible set of symbols with which we can count and perform arithmetic. Most of the difficulties in understanding the binary system result from this simplicity. Figure 3.1 represents the relation between a group of four electronic cells and various number systems.

Electronic Cells	Binary	Decimal	Hexadecimal
	0 0 0 0	0	0
	0 0 0 1	1	1
	0 0 1 0	2	2
	0 0 1 1	3	3
	0 1 0 0	4	4
	0 1 0 1	5	5
	0 1 1 0	6	6
	0 1 1 1	7	7
	1 0 0 0	8	8
	1 0 0 1	9	9
	1 0 1 0	10	A
	1 0 1 1	11	B
	1 1 0 0	12	C
	1 1 0 1	13	D
	1 1 1 0	14	E
	1 1 1 1	15	F

Figure 3.1 Electronic Cells and Number Systems

Note that the binary numbers in Figure 3.1 match the physical state of the electronic cell. If we think of each cell as a miniature light bulb, then the binary number 1 can be used to represent the state of a charged cell (light bulb on) and the binary number 0 to represent the state of an uncharged cell (light bulb off). In this sense we often say that a *bit is set* if its binary value is 1 and that a *bit is reset*, or clear, if its binary value is 0. Binary numbers in Figure 3.1 are followed by the letter B, which is the way in which binaries are entered in 80x86 assembly language.

Hexadecimal Numbers

The column to the right of the binary numbers in Figure 3.1 holds the conventional decimal representation and the rightmost column the hexadecimal representation. Hexadecimal numbers are convenient because they a provide a shorthand for representing binary numbers. The hexadecimal shorthand has proved particularly useful because most modern computers use memory cells, registers, and data paths in multiples of four binary digits. In Figure 3.1 we can see that all possible combinations of four binary digits can be encoded in a single hexadecimal digit. Hexadecimal numbers are sometimes called hex.

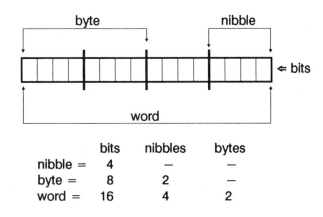

	bits	nibbles	bytes
nibble =	4	—	—
byte =	8	2	—
word =	16	4	2

Figure 3.2 Common Units Used in Measuring Memory

Units of Memory Storage

The assembly language programmer often uses memory to store and retrieve data and instructions. In order to access memory, the programmer must become familiar with the units of memory measurement. Some of the smaller memory units are shown in Figure 3.2.

The smallest unit of memory measurement is called the *bit*. The term bit is derived from the words BInary digiT. The *nibble* consists of 4 bits. A *byte* contains two nibbles (8 bits) and a *word* contains 2 bytes (16 bits). In the IBM microcomputers the smallest unit of memory that can be directly stored or retrieved is 1 byte.

The bits contained in a memory storage unit are numbered from right to left; the rightmost bit is designated bit number 0. Figure 3.3 shows the bit numbers in a byte-size storage unit.

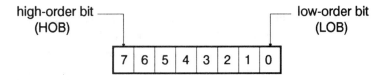

Figure 3.3 Bit Numbering in a Byte Unit

3.1 CONVERSIONS

The 80x86 assembly language programmer regularly works with three different number systems: decimal, binary, and hexadecimal. Therefore, a need often arises for converting values from any one of these systems into another one. Assembler programs provide a first level of assistance in number systems conversions by allowing the programmer to enter values encoded in any one of these systems. Most 80x86 commercial assemblers, including Microsoft's MASM and Intel's ASM 86, recognize the letter B as an identifier for a binary number and the letter H for a hexadecimal numbers. Decimal values are entered either without a trailing letter or by using the letter D. For example, the instructions:

```
MOV     AL,176          ; Input is in decimal
MOV     AL,176D         ; Input is also decimal
MOV     AL,10110000B    ; Input is in binary
MOV     AL,0B0H         ; Input is in hexadecimal
```

Note that the hexadecimal value in the last instruction is preceded with a 0. The 0 is used if the first digit of the hexadecimal number is an A, B, C, D, E, or F. In this case the leading 0 is necessary in order to inform the assembler that the value is a hexadecimal number and not a label or variable name.

Many inexpensive calculators provide binary and hexadecimal conversions. Also available on the market are specialized programmers' calculators that have many other logic and arithmetic operations used in the computer world, in addition to number systems conversions.

Although calculators are convenient, longhand conversions of numbers in the decimal, binary, and hexadecimal systems are quite simple. The conversion from binary to hexadecimal and vice versa can be performed by simple inspection or by using a four-digit table such as the one in Figure 3.1. This table can be easily reconstructed by observing that the binary values 0 and 1 change every other digit in the rightmost column, every two digits in the next column to the left, every four digits in the next one, and every eight digits in the leftmost column.

Conversions from binary to decimal and decimal to binary are based on the positional value (relative weight) of each digit. In any number system the positional value of each digit is obtained by raising the digit position to consecutive integer powers of the base of the number system (also called the radix). For example, in the decimal system (base 10) the positional weight of the digits are the integer powers of 10 starting at the rightmost digit. In the binary number system the positional weight of the digits are the consecutive integer powers of 2. Figure 3.4 shows the use of the binary digit weights in converting a binary number into its decimal equivalent.

Converting from decimal to binary is performed by finding the next smaller column weight, entering a binary 1 in that column position, and subtracting the column weight. The method is shown in the example of Figure 3.5.

In Figure 3.5, the next smaller column weight for the number 179 is bit position number 7, with a weight of 128. A binary 1 is entered in for this bit position, then 128 is subtracted from 179 leaving a remainder of 51. Now the next smaller column weight for

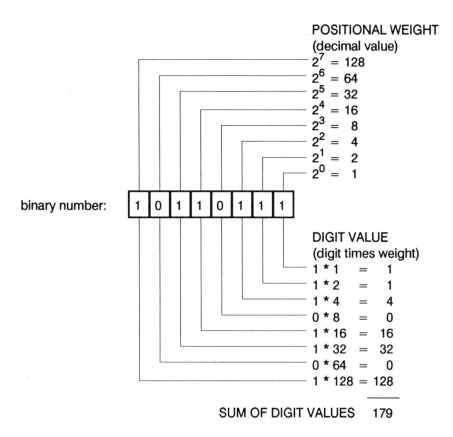

Figure 3.4 Converting a Binary to a Decimal Number

the number 51 is bit position number 5, with a weight of 32. A 1 digit is entered for this bit postion, 32 is subtrated from 51, and the process continues until the remainder is zero.

In assembly language programs conversion of decimal numbers to binary and vice versa is not usually performed using the methods described for longhand conversions. This is because data are stored in memory and registers in binary form and also to the availability of microprocessor instructions that facilitate the conversions. The program LESSON3.ASM listed at the end of this chapter contains a conversion routine for displaying the bits in a decimal number.

3.2 CHARACTER REPRESENTATION

Computer data stored in memory or machine registers are represented by a pattern of electrical cells that hold either a binary 1 or a binary 0. We have seen that binary numbers can be used for counting, much like decimal numbers; therefore, it is easy to understand

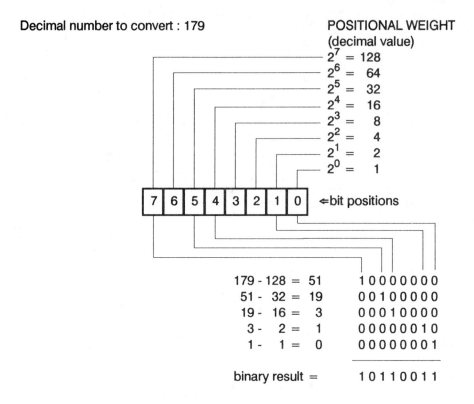

Decimal number to convert : 179

POSITIONAL WEIGHT
(decimal value)
2^7 = 128
2^6 =   64
2^5 =   32
2^4 =   16
2^3 =   8
2^2 =   4
2^1 =   2
2^0 =   1

| 7 | 6 | 5 | 4 | 3 | 2 | 1 | 0 | ⇐bit positions

179 - 128 =	51	1 0 0 0 0 0 0 0
51 - 32 =	19	0 0 1 0 0 0 0 0
19 - 16 =	3	0 0 0 1 0 0 0 0
3 - 2 =	1	0 0 0 0 0 0 1 0
1 - 1 =	0	0 0 0 0 0 0 0 1

binary result =   1 0 1 1 0 0 1 1

Figure 3.5 Converting a Decimal to a Binary Number

that a number can be stored in a computer system using a binary code. Because these patterns of 1's and 0's provide the most convenient way of representing computer information, character data are also stored in this manner.

A code is a correspondence scheme between symbols and letters of the alphabet and the digits of a number system. For example, if we agree that the letter A is represented by the number 1, the letter B by the number 2, and so forth, to the letter Z, represented by the number 26, then we can encode text messages using numbers instead of letters. In this case, the letters IBM would be represented by the numbers 9 2 13. Historically, several methods of representing character data have been used in computer technology, such as the Hollerith code used in punched cards and the Extended Binary Coded Decimal Interchange Code, known as EBCDIC.

In recent years the American Standard Code for Information Interchange, or ASCII (pronounced as-key), has gained almost universal acceptance. The IBM micro-computers use the ASCII encoding for text and symbols. Appendix C contains a table of the ASCII codes in the IBM character set.

3.3 THE 80x86 MICROPROCESSOR

The IBM and IBM-compatible microcomputers are equipped with Intel microprocessors of the iAPX family. Table 3.1 shows the use of Intel chips in the various lines and models of IBM microcomputers.

TABLE 3.1 USE OF INTEL MICROPROCESSORS IN IBM MICROCOMPUTERS

Intel Processor	PC LINE				PS/2 LINE		
	PC & PC XT	PCJR	PC AT XT 286	Model 25 Model 30	Model 50 Model 60	Model 70 Model 80	Model 90
8088	X	X					
8086				X			
80286			X		X		
80386						X	
80486						X*	X

* Optional in the model 70-A21 with removable processor card

The 8086 and the 8088 microprocessors appear identical to the programmer. The difference between these chips is related to the width of the communications lines (buses) and to how memory data are accessed. Other Intel microprocessors of the iAPX family are *upward compatible* with the 8086 and the 8088. This means that more advanced chips, like the 80286, can execute all the instructions and operations of the 8086 and the 8088. But these later model chips also have additional instructions and features that do not exist in their predecessors. In other words, programs developed for the 8086 or 8088 will execute on the 80286, 80386, or the 486, but programs that use the features of a more advanced processor will not run on an earlier chip. The advanced features of the 80286, 80386, and 484 microprocessors will not be discussed in this book.

80x86 Architecture

A microprocessor is an electronic device that performs operations on data according to an internal *instruction set*. Each instruction in this set is recognized by its operation code. The 80x86 chip is divided internally into two separate units of execution. The *bus interface unit* (BIU) fetches the operation codes from memory and places them in an internal waiting line, called a *queue*. The *execution unit* (EU) decodes and executes the instructions in this queue.

The 8086 and the 8088 microprocessors contain 14 internal registers. Other processors of the iAPX family have other internal registers in addition to this basic set. The registers can be classified into four groups: the general purpose registers, the index and pointer registers, the segment registers, and the status and control registers. Figure 3.6 is a programmer's view of the 8086 and the 8088 CPU.

GENERAL PURPOSE REGISTERS

AH	AL	AX
BH	BL	BX
CH	CL	CX
DH	DL	DX

INDEX AND POINTER REGISTERS

stack pointer	SP
base pointer	BP
source index	SI
destination index	DI

SEGMENT REGISTERS

code segment	CS
data segment	DS
stack segment	SS
extra segment	ES

CONTROL AND STATUS REGISTERS

instruction pointer	IP
flags register	

Figure 3.6 Programmer's View of the 80x86 Microprocessor

The General Purpose Registers

The general purpose registers are also called the *data registers*. Each of the four data registers can hold 16 bits of information. The upper and lower half of the data registers can be addressed independently. Therefore, we can code

```
        MOV     AL,12           ; Load the value 12 into AL
```

and

```
        MOV     AX,1234         ; Load 1234 into AX
```

However, we cannot code

```
MOV     AL,1234         ; Impossible operation
```

This last instruction is not possible, because the AL register can hold only 8 bits of information, and the largest decimal number that can be represented in 8 binary digits is 255.

The data registers are used in arithmetic and logical operations and in performing data transfers. In most cases it is up to the programmer to determine which general purpose register is used, although a few 80x86 instructions require the use of specific registers.

The Index and Pointer Registers

The *index* and *pointer registers* are called stack pointer (SP), base pointer (BP), source index (SI), and destination index (DI). Although these registers can be used in arithmetic and logical operations, they are more frequently destined to hold addresses than data. The two pointer registers, SP and BP, provide easy access to items located in the stack area. SI and DI, named the index registers, are typically used in accessing items located in the data area. SI and DI are used implicitly by some 80x86 instructions.

The Segment Registers

The *segment registers* are the 16-bit registers named code segment (CS), data segment (DS), stack segment (SS), and extra segment (ES). These registers are used in the segmented memory architecture of the 80x86 microprocessors. The 80x86 memory structure is discussed in Lesson3.ASM

Instructions reside in the code segment and are addressed through the CS register. The offset of the instruction is determined by the instruction pointer register. Program data are usually located in the data segment, addressed through the DS register. The stack is addressed through the SS register. The extra segment register, as the name implies, can be used to address operands, data, memory, and other items outside the current data and stack segments. Many assembly language programs for the IBM microcomputers use the ES register as a pointer into video display memory (see Chapter 5).

The Control and Status Registers

The *instruction pointer* (IP) register serves to locate the beginning of the next instruction to be executed. In previous generations of microprocessors this register was called the *program counter*. This register is managed by the CPU and cannot be changed directly by the programmer.

The *flag register* holds 3 control and 6 status bits, called the *flags*. Figure 3.7 shows the locations of the individual flag bits in the 80x86 flags register.

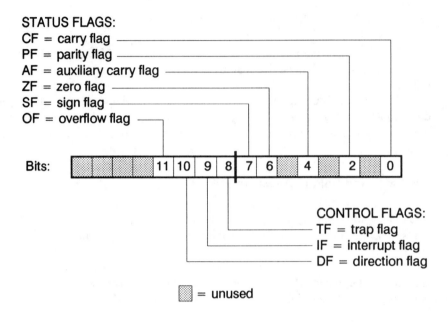

Figure 3.7 80x86 Flags Register

The control flags allow changing the operation of the microprocessor in specific ways. For example, the state of the interrupt flag (IF) determines if hardware interrupts will be recognized by the CPU or if they will be ignored. The direction flag (DF), used in some string instructions, determines if data moves proceed from low to high addresses or vice versa. The trap flag (TF) is used mostly by debugger programs.

Each status flag bit records a property of the result of the previous instruction executed by the CPU. For example, after the operation

```
SUB     AX,AX               ; AX - AX = 0
```

the zero flag will be set because the results of subtracting a value from itself is zero. Table 3.2 shows the functions of the 80x86 status flags.

3.4 NEW ELEMENTS IN THE PROGRAM LESSON3.ASM

The program LESSON3.ASM converts a single-digit decimal number input by the user to binary and displays four binary digits. The program uses two MS-DOS services discussed in LESSON2.ASM, as well as several new program elements.

TABLE 3.2 80X86 STATUS FLAGS

BIT	FLAG NAME	CODE	FUNCTION
11	Overflow	OF	Set to show arithmetic overflow
7	Sign	SF	In signed arithmetic SF shows if the result is positive (SF = 0) or negative (SF = 1)
6	Zero	ZF	Set if the result of the previous operation is zero
4	Auxiliary carry	AF	In decimal arithmetic AF shows if there is a carry out of the low nibble or a borrow from the high nibble
2	Parity	PF	Set if the result of the previous operation has produced an even number of 1-bits (used mostly in data transmissions)
0	Carry	CF	Set if there is a carry or a borrow to the high-order bit of the result; also used by rotate instructions

Obtaining a Keyboard Character

BIOS service number 0 of interrupt 16H provides a convenient way for an assembly language program to obtain a keyboard character typed by the user (see text reference # 1 in LESSON3.ASM). This service waits until a key is pressed; therefore, control does not return to the program until the user touches one of the keys. The ASCII code for the key that was pressed is placed by the service in the AL register.

ASCII to Binary Conversion

The keystroke returned by service number 0, interrupt 16H, is encoded in the ASCII format (see Appendix C). This means that if the user pressed the keyboard key labeled with the number 5, the AL register holds the ASCII code 35H. Note that the numbers 0 to 9 are sequentially located in the table, as follows:

Number	ASCII code
0	30H
1	31H
2	32H
.	
.	
9	39H

For this reason, the conversion of a single-digit ASCII decimal number to binary is performed by subtracting the value 30H from the ASCII code (see text reference # 2 in LESSON3.ASM).

Using the Stack

In Chapter 2 we mentioned an auxiliary data structure called the stack. Programs use the stack in many different ways. One of the common uses of this area is to temporarily store data so as to liberate machine registers for other uses. Because the 80x86 has only four general purpose registers, programs quite frequently must save registers in the stack. The PUSH instruction places the operand on the current stack position, determined by the SP (stack pointer) register. This position is often called the stack top. The POP instruction restores in the operand the value currently at the *stack top.*

Stack mismanagement is a frequent source of program errors. The analogy mentioned in Chapter 2 between a coin dispenser and a stack structure indicates that the programmer must keep track of how items are placed in the stack so that they can be correctly restored. For example, the sequence

```
PUSH    AX              ; AX to stack top
PUSH    BX              ; BX to stack top
PUSH    CX              ; CX to stack top
```

places the contents of AX, BX, and CX on the stack. Because the last element pushed is the first one to come out, the sequence for restoring the original registers will be as follows:

```
POP     CX              ; Stack top to CX
POP     BX              ; Stack top to BX
POP     AX              ; Stack top to AX
```

Many programmers make it a habit to push registers on the stack in alphabetical order. The correct POP sequence can be easily derived by reversing this order.

In the program LESSON3.ASM we must save the keystroke input by the user and placed in AL by BIOS service number 0, interrupt 16H (see text reference # 3) before we use the MS-DOS string display service. This is necessary because MS-DOS service request 9, interrupt 21H, uses the AX register for its own purposes. A PUSH/POP sequence, shown in LESSON3.ASM, uses the stack to save and restore the value in AX. Note that to save AL we must use the instruction PUSH AX, because PUSH and POP act on double registers. The instruction PUSH AL does not exist.

Program Loops

Computer programs must often repeat an operation or a sequence of operations. A *loop* is a programming structure that performs this repetition. All programming languages have facilities for executing loops. Loops can be implemented using several techniques. Perhaps the most common one is based on the 80x86 LOOP instruction. The following skeleton code contains the elements of a loop:

```
        MOV     CX,8            ; Initialize counter register
                                ; for 8 iterations
REPEAT_POINT:
        .
        .
        LOOP    REPEAT_POINT    ; Loop to operand label
```

The components of this program skeleton are as follows:

1. An instruction that initializes the CX register to the number of iterations to be executed in the loop.

2. A label (REPEAT_POINT) that marks the beginning of the loop.

3. A LOOP instruction that references the loop label.

The initialization step is related to the operation of the LOOP instruction, which decrements the CX register and transfers execution to an operand label if decrementing CX did not make it zero. Note that the initialization of CX must be performed *outside* the loop. If the initialization instruction is placed inside the loop, then the loop will never end because the value of CX would be reentered on every iteration. The program LESSON3.ASM contains the loop label TEST_LEFT_BIT (see text reference # 4 in LESSON3.ASM).

Testing Bits

The TEST instruction (see text reference # 5 in LESSON3.ASM) is used to compare the source and the destination operand without changing its contents. For example, in LESSON3.ASM the test instruction is

```
        TEST    AH,00001000B    ; Test AH bit 3
```

In this case the source operand is a binary value in which bit number 3 is set (see the bit numbering in Figure 3.3). Bit patterns such as this one, often called a *bit mask*, are used in programming to preserve the value of one or more bits of the source operand. The test instruction will give a nonzero result if the destination operand contains 1-bits that match the 1-bits in the mask. In this case, if the contents of the AH register was a value in which bit number 3 was set, the result of the test instruction will not be zero.

Conditional Jumps

We have said that the result of a TEST instruction is not zero if there are matching 1-bits in both operands. In the example in LESSON3.ASM (see text reference # 5) the result of the TEST instruction will be not zero if bit number 3 of the AH register is 1. Recall from Section 3.2 that the zero flag of the 80x86 status register is set if the result of the previous operation is zero. By the same token, the zero flag is clear if the result of a previous operation is not zero.

The 80x86 *conditional jump* instructions allow the program to direct execution according to the state of the various flag registers. For example, the JNZ (jump if not zero) instruction transfers execution to the operand label if the result of the previous operation was not zero. In the program LESSON3.ASM we use the JNZ instruction to direct execution to the label LEFT_BIT_SET if the TEST instruction that precedes it produced a nonzero result.

The rule to remember regarding bit testing is that the conditional jump (JNZ) following the TEST instruction will be taken if there are 1-bits in the destination operand that match the 1-bits in the mask.

Procedures

All programming languages provide ways for simplifying the source code by creating subprograms. Subprograms are also known as *modules, procedures, functions*, or *subroutines*. Typically a subprogram contains operations that are executed more than once in the program. By providing a single encoding for a routine used more than once, the subprogram saves development time and storage space. Subprograms are called *procedures* in 80x86 assembly language.

The program LESSON3.ASM contains a procedure named TTY (see text reference # 7). The letters TTY, shorthand for the word "teletype," were chosen because this procedure uses BIOS service number 14, interrupt 10H, sometimes called the BIOS teletype service. The TTY procedure displays the character contained in the AL register. Note that we have used comment lines to list the entry and exit conditions of the TTY procedure.

Procedures are created using the PROC and ENDP assembler directives. A procedure skeleton in 80x86 assembly language is as follows:

```
PROC_NAME          PROC      NEAR/FAR
          .

          .
          RET
PROC_NAME          ENDP
```

The following program elements are found in this skeleton.

1. The PROC assembler directive creates a procedure named by the programmer (PROC_NAME). 80x86 procedures can be of the types NEAR or FAR. These terms, which are related to the procedure's placement in 80x86 segmented memory, will be explained in Chapter 4.

2. The ENDP directive serves to mark the end of a procedure.

3. Procedures are executed through the CALL instruction. For example, to execute the skeleton procedure listed above, the programmer would code

```
CALL      PROC_NAME
```

4. The RET instruction is used inside the procedure to return control to the calling routine. After the RET instruction execution resumes at the line that follows the corresponding CALL.

Shifting Bits

In the program LESSON3.ASM we must examine the four low-order bits of the decimal number entered by the user. Although there are many ways in which this can be performed, perhaps the most convenient one is by shifting the bits in either the mask or the user's input. The 80x86 SHL (shift left) instruction is used to move each bit one position to the left. In this manner, after performing SHL, bit 0 takes the position of bit 1, bit 1 the position of bit 2, and so on. In a left shift the high-order bit (bit 7) is discarded and a 0 is shifted into the bit-0-position. This action is shown in Figure 3.8.

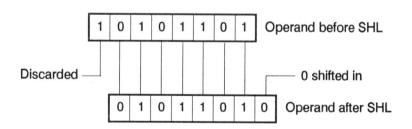

Figure 3.8 Example of the Action of the SHL Instruction

In LESSON3.ASM (see text reference # 8) the SHL instruction is used to shift left all the bits in the AH register. Because AH contains the binary value of the user's input, the shift, test, and display sequence provides a simple way of obtaining the binary equivalent of a decimal number.

3.5 SOURCE CODE LISTING OF THE PROGRAM LESSON3.ASM

```
;******************************************************************
;******************************************************************
;                              LESSON3.ASM
;******************************************************************
;******************************************************************
; Program title: LESSON3
; Start date:
; Last modification:
;
; Program description:
; Convert a decimal digit, input by the user, to binary and
; display
;
; New operations:
; 1. Obtain a keyboard character
; 2. Convert an ASCII character to binary
; 3. Test and display bits
;
;******************************************************************
;                              stack segment
;******************************************************************
STACK   SEGMENT stack
;
                DB      1024 DUP ('?')  ; Default stack is 1K
STACK   ENDS
;
;******************************************************************
;                              data segment
;******************************************************************
DATA    SEGMENT
;
DIGIT_MESS      DB      'Type one decimal digit: $'
BINARY_MESS     DB      0AH,0DH,'Binary value is: $'
;
DATA    ENDS
;******************************************************************
;                              code segment
;******************************************************************
;
CODE    SEGMENT
```

```
        ASSUME  CS:CODE
;*******************|
;  initialization   |
;*******************|
ENTRY_POINT:
; Initialize the DS register so that the program can access the
; data items in this segment
        MOV     AX,DATA         ; Address of DATA to AX
        MOV     DS,AX           ; and to DS
        ASSUME  DS:DATA         ; Assume directive so that
                                ; the assembler defaults to DS
;*********************|
;    display first    |
;      message        |
;*********************|
; Display a message stored in the data segment using DOS service
; number 9, INT 21H. The message must end in a $ sign
        LEA     DX,DIGIT_MESS   ; Set DX to message test
        MOV     AH,9            ; Service request number
        INT     21H             ; Transfer control to MS DOS
;                               |*********************|
;                               | text reference # 1 |
;                               |*********************|
;*********************|
;  wait for keystroke |
;*********************|
; The program uses BIOS service number 0, INT 16H, to wait until
; a key is pressed. This service has no entry requirements
        MOV     AH,0            ; Service request number
        INT     16H             ; Transfer control to BIOS
; Service number 0 of interrupt 16H, returns in AL the ASCII code
; for the key pressed.
;                               |*********************|
;                               | text reference # 2 |
;                               |*********************|
;*********************|
;   convert to binary |
;*********************|
; The program assumes that the key was a number key in the range
; 0 to 9. The ASCII value is converted to binary by subtracting
; 30H
        SUB     AL,30H          ; Subtract 30H from keystroke
```

```
;
;*********************|
;    display second   |
;        message      |
;*********************|
;                                      |********************|
;                                      | text reference # 3 |
;                                      |********************|
; AL holds the binary value of the user's input. This register is
; saved on the stack
        PUSH    AX              ; Save AL in stack
; Display message
        LEA     DX,BINARY_MESS  ; Set DX to message text
        MOV     AH,9            ; Service request number
        INT     21H             ; Transfer control to MS DOS
        POP     AX              ; Recover binary from stack
;*********************|
;    display binary   |
;*********************|
; Bits are examined form left to right. If the bit is set a
; 1 is displayed. If not, a 0 is displayed
        MOV     AH,AL           ; Bits to AH. AL is needed to
                                ; hold character to be displayed
;                                      |********************|
;                                      | text reference # 4 |
;                                      |********************|
        MOV     CX,4            ; Set up loop counter for 4 bits
TEST_LEFT_BIT:
;                                      |********************|
;                                      | text reference # 5 |
;                                      |********************|
        TEST    AH,00001000B    ; Test AH bit 3
;                                      |********************|
;                                      | text reference # 6 |
;                                      |********************|
        JNZ     LEFT_BIT_SET    ; Jump is taken if bit 3 is set
; At this point bit 3 is not set. Display a 0
        MOV     AL,'0'          ; Character to be displayed
        CALL    TTY             ; Procedure to display
        JMP     NEXT_BIT        ; Go to shift and continue
; Display a 1 if bit number 3 is set
LEFT_BIT_SET:
```

```
            MOV     AL,'1'              ; Character to be displayed
            CALL    TTY                 ; Local display procedure
;*********************|
;  shift left AH bits |
;*********************|
NEXT_BIT:
;                                       |********************|
;                                       |  text reference # 8 |
;                                       |********************|
            SHL     AH,1                ; Bits in AH are shifted left
                                        ; one position
            LOOP    TEST_LEFT_BIT       ; Continue until CX = 0
;******************|
;   exit to DOS    |
;******************|
; After the message is displayed the program gives back control
; to MS DOS using service number 76
DOS_EXIT:
            MOV     AH,76               ; DOS service request code
            MOV     AL,0                ; No error code returned
            INT     21H                 ; TO DOS
;****************************************************************
;                        procedures
;****************************************************************
;                                       |********************|
;                                       |  text reference # 7 |
;                                       |********************|
TTY     PROC    NEAR
; Local procedure to display a character using BIOS teletype
; service number 14 of INT 10H
; On entry:
;          AL = ASCII character to be displayed
; On exit:
;          nothing
;          AX is preserved
;
            PUSH    AX                  ; Save AX in stack
            MOV     AH,14               ; Service request number
            MOV     BX,0                ; Display page is usually 0
            INT     10H                 ; BIOS video service interrupt
            POP     AX                  ; Restore AX from stack
            RET                         ; End of procedure
```

```
TTY       ENDP
;**************************************************************
CODE      ENDS
          END     ENTRY_POINT    ; Reference to label at which
                                 ; execution starts
```

VOCABULARY

binary system	instruction set
bit mask	interrupt flag
bit reset	keystroke returned
bit set	loop
bus interface unit	memory
byte	module
conditional jump	nibble
control & status registers	procedure
data registers	queue
direction flag	segment registers
flag	stack
flag register	stack pointer register
function	subroutine
hexadecimal	trap flag
index & pointer registers	upward compatible
instruction pointer register	word

QUESTIONS

1. What is the positional value of each digit in the decimal number 12358?
2. How many symbols are used in the binary system of numbers?
3. A bit holding a value of binary one is said to be set or reset?
4. What is the use of hexadecimal numbers?
5. How many nibbles are in 1 byte?
6. How many bits are in 1 nibble?
7. Conver the binary number 10010001B to decimal using the weight of each digit column.
8. Convert the decimal number 1991 to binary using the weight of each digit column.
9. What words form the acronym ASCII?
10. List the four general purpose registers in the Intel 80x86 microprocessors.
11. List the four segment registers in the Intel 80x86 microprocessors.
12. What is the purpose of the instruction pointer (IP) register?

13. When is the zero flag set?

EXERCISES

1. Modify the program LESSON3.ASM so that keystrokes outside the valid range (number keys 0 to 9) are detected and ignored.
2. Write a flowchart for the decimal-to-binary conversion routine in the program LESSON3.ASM.
3. Write a version of the program LESSON3.ASM that displays the eight binary digits in the ASCII value of any keystroke.

4

Memory and Addressing Modes, BIOS, and Logic

4.0 THE 80x86 MEMORY SPACE

It is a historical fact that the development of the 8086 and other similar microprocessors was spurred by the need for more memory. The 6502, 8080, Z-80, and other 8-bit microcomputer chips of the previous generation could address 64 kilobytes of memory (65,535 bytes). As system and application programs grew larger and more elaborate, these 64K became insufficient to hold programs and user data. But designing and building a microprocessor with larger memory addressing capabilities entailed some practical considerations. The 8086 resulted from efforts by Intel Corporation to produce a machine with expanded capabilities without exceeding certain practical limits regarding the cost of the microprocessor and of the resulting microcomputer.

The problem of addressing a larger memory space is directly related to the hardware elements that must hold the memory addresses. If we recall that four binary digits are encoded in one hexadecimal digit, we see that the largest number that can be stored in a 4-bit computer cell corresponds with the hexadecimal digit F (Figure 3.1). This means that in a computer system using 16 bits to encode memory addresses, the largest memory address is represented by the digits FFFFH. In other words, the addressing limit of the 64K microprocessors results from the use of 16-bit registers.

A simple way to build a microprocessor with a larger memory space would be to enlarge the machine registers and other hardware elements accordingly. For example, by adding four binary digits to the memory addressing hardware, the maximum capabilities would be expanded to FFFFFH (1,048,575) bytes. However, cost and other hardware and software considerations advised against building a 20-bit computer.

Segmented Memory

The solution adopted by Intel in the design of the 8086 (chronologically the first member of the 80x86 family) was to retain the 8- and 16-bit registers of the previous generation of microprocessors and expand the memory addressing capabilities by combining two 16-bit registers to form a 20-bit address. This scheme, known as *segmented memory*, provides a practical way for increasing the machine's memory space without excessively increasing development and manufacturing cost.

The logic behind the segmented memory scheme is as follows: one 16-bit register (called the *segment register*) is used to locate the start of a 64K block of memory in the machine's 1024K (1 megabyte) memory space. A second 16-bit register (called the *offset register*) is used to locate the individual memory bytes within this 64K segment. Figure 4.1 shows the location of a memory item using a segment and an offset register.

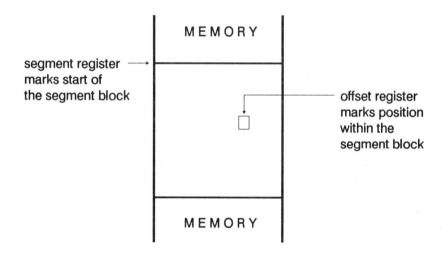

Figure 4.1 Segmented Memory Addressing Scheme

Physical and Logical Addresses

In a segmented memory computer, in order to locate an item stored in the memory location at address A0008H we set a 16-bit segment register to the value A000H and an offset register to the value 0008H. The actual register arithmetic in this example is as follows:

```
          Segment register    A 0 0 0    H
      +   Offset register        0 0 8 H

          Address             A 0 0 0 8 H
```

Observe that, before performing the addition operation, the value in the segment register is shifted left 4 bits (one hexadecimal digit). The resulting sum is a 20-bit *physical address*.

The term "physical address" represents the actual memory location, whereas *logical address* is used to represent the two 16-bit elements that form it. The logical address is often written with the segment and the offset component separated by a semicolon, for example:

```
physical address = A0008H
logical address  = A000:0008H
```

The advantage of using a logical address is that it represents the actual values that must be loaded into the segment and the offset registers.

Initializing the Segment Register

We have seen that in order for an 80x86 program to access data it must use two registers, segment and offset. The segment registers, briefly mentioned in Section 3.3, are named the stack segment (SS), the code segment (CS), the data segment (DS), and the extra segment (ES). These segment registers are shown in Figure 3.6.

The first function performed by the programs LESSON2.ASM and LESSON3.ASM, listed in Chapters 2 and 3, as well as by most programs in this book, is to *initialize* the data segment register. Until the data segment register is set to the start of the segment block, the data items contained in this memory area cannot be accessed by the program. The actual initialization lines are as follows:

```
; Initialize the DS register so that the program can access the
; data items in this segment
        MOV     AX,DATA         ; Address of DATA to AX
        MOV     DS,AX           ; and to DS
        ASSUME  DS:DATA         ; Assume directive so that
                                ; the assembler defaults to DS
```

In this case the assembler locates the beginning of the data segment using a name (DATA) assigned by the programmer when the segment was created. If the programmer had used a different segment name while creating the segment, for example,

```
MY_DAT  SEGMENT
          .
          .
MY_DAT  ENDS
```

then the segment register initialization instructions would be

```
MOV     AX,MY_DAT
MOV     DS,AX
ASSUME  DS:MY_DAT
```

Also note that the DS register is loaded via the AX register. This is necessary because the 80x86, for reasons of code economy, does not allow immediate operands with segment registers. In other words, the following instruction is not legal:

```
MOV     DS,MY_DAT        ; Illegal operand
```

The ASSUME Directive

The last line of the initialization routines listed above is

```
ASSUME  DS:MY_DAT
```

ASSUME is a directive that informs the assembler which segment to use as a default. It is by virtue of the ASSUME statement that, in many instructions, the segment element of the address is transparent to the program. For example, the instruction

```
LEA     DX,MESSAGE_1     ; Set DX to message test
```

sets DX as a pointer to a item in the data segment. The programmer need not specify the segment register to be used, because the ASSUME statement has instructed the assembler program what segment register and value to use. On the other hand, the following instructions can be seen at the start of the code segment of all programs in this book:

```
CODE    SEGMENT
        ASSUME  CS:CODE
```

In this case the ASSUME statement informs the assembler to use the CS and the address of the segment name CODE as a default for all code operations. Therefore, in calculating jumps, calls, and other code segment operations the assembler will use CS = CODE as a default. Later in this chapter we will see how the programmer can override these default segment assignments whenever it is necessary.

4.1 80x86 ADDRESSING MODES

The location of an operand is called the *operand address*. In the 80x86 microprocessor the following elements can serve as instruction operands: microprocessor registers, immediate values, memory locations, and ports.

In the previous chapters we have used registers and values as operands of instructions. For instance, in the instruction

```
MOV     AH,9              ; Load 9 into AH
```

we can identify a register (AH) and an immediate operand (the value 9). In these first programs we have also used memory operands; for example, in LESSON3.ASM the instruction

```
LEA     DX,DIGIT_MESS    ; Set DX to message test
```

refers to the address of a data item named DIGIT_MESS. In addition, also in LESSON3.ASM, the instruction

```
JNZ     LEFT_BIT_SET     ; Jump is taken if bit 3 is set
```

transfers execution to a memory address identified by the label LEFT_BIT_SET. Therefore, we have already used three of the four operand types in the 80x86. Ports are input/output facilities of the 80x86 and will be discussed in Chapter 9.

The various ways of identifying an operand are called the addressing modes. *Addressing modes* for *register* and *immediate* operands are simple. Register operands are addressed using the register names. Some 80x86 instructions allow addressing the 8-bit portions of a machine register, for example:

```
MOV     CL,21
```

or the entire 16-bit register, for example:

```
MOV     AX,1234
```

There are no addressing options for immediate operands, although we have seen that the assembler program allows representing immediate values in decimal, binary, and hexadecimal notation. Table 4.1 presents a description of the most commonly used addressing modes in the 80x86 microprocessors.

4.2 MEMORY ADDRESSING

Reference to a machine register is always interpreted to mean the register's contents; for example, the instruction

```
MOV     AL,AH
```

consists of copying the contents of the AH register into AL. On the other hand, a reference to a memory location can relate to either its address its contents.

In order to access the contents of a memory operand, the 80x86 must know the two address elements: the segment and the offset. The segment determination is usually performed according to the type of instruction and the applicable ASSUME statement, although the programmer can override the assumption and request a specific segment register. The offset portion of the operand's address (known as the *effective address*) is determined according to the memory addressing mode used in the operand. For example, a program can read the contents of a memory location at a specific address, as follows:

```
MOV     AX,[140H]
```

This instruction loads the AX register with the contents of the memory location at offset 140H in the currently assumed data segment register. The bracket symbols enclosing the address portion of the operand are called the *indirection indicators*. These symbols signal to the assembler that it is the *contents of* location 140H that must be loaded into AX and not the immediate value 140H.

TABLE 4.1 MOST COMMON 80X86 ADDRESSING MODES

MODE	EXAMPLE	DESCRIPTION
Register	MOV **AL,21**	Operand is a CPU register
Immediate	MOV **AL,21**	Operand is a value
Direct	MOV **AX,[40H]**	Operand is the contents of a memory location speficied by its address
Indirect	MOV **[SI],AX**	Operand is the contents of a memory location specified in the registers BX, SI, or DI
Based	MOV **AX,[BX+6]**	Operand is the contents of amemory location specified using the BX or BP registers and a displacement value
Indexed	MOV **AX,[SI+4]**	Operand is the contents of a memory location specified using the SI or DI registers and a displacement

Direct Addressing

Direct addressing takes place when a offset element of a memory location is referred specifically in the operand, as in the example in Figure 4.1. Direct addressing also takes place if the item is represented by its variable name; for example, the instruction

```
MOV      AL,[BYTE_ITEM]
```

loads the AL register with the contents of the byte-size memory variable named BYTE_ITEM. However, in this case the bracket symbols are superfluous because the assembler assumes that a reference to a variable always means the contents of the variable. Recall from Chapters 2 and 3 that the offset of the variable is obtained with the LEA instruction. This means that the above instruction is more frequently coded in the form

```
MOV      AL,BYTE_ITEM.
```

Indirect Addressing

Although direct addressing finds frequent use in 80x86 assembly language programs, there are times when other memory addressing modes are more convenient. For example, in the program LESSON4.ASM listed at the end of this chapter we use BIOS service number 14 of interrupt 10H to display each of the characters in a text message (see text reference #1). In this case direct addressing would have required calculating the physical memory offset of each character in the string.

In order to simplify processing of multiple data items, a program can set a processor register as a pointer to one of the items in the set and access other items by manipulating this pointer. When the procedure DISPLAY_MSG in LESSON4.ASM (see text reference # 1) received control, the SI register pointed to the first character in a string of characters to be displayed. The individual characters are moved to the AL register with the instruction

```
MOV      AL,[SI]          ; Message character to AL
```

(see text reference # 2). Note the use of the indirection indicators (brackets) to specify *the contents of the memory location pointed at by SI*. A few lines later (see text reference # 3) the program *bumps the pointer* to the next character in the string. This is done by means of the INC (increment) instruction.

Not all registers can be used as pointers to memory data. The ones that can be used as pointers are the *index registers* (SI and DI) and the *base registers* (BX and BP). Pointers can also be used to store items in memory, as in the example of indirect addressing in Table 4.1.

Based and Indexed Addressing

The index and base registers, SI, DI, BX, and BP, also allow adding a displacement to the contents of the pointer register. These addressing modes are called *based addressing* if the base registers BX or BP are used as operands, or *indexed addressing* if the index registers SI or DI are used. The simplest form of based and indexed addressing is shown in Figure 4.1.

4.3 LOGICAL INSTRUCTIONS

The microprocessors of the 80x86 family can perform bit-by-bit manipulations by means of several *logical instructions*. These instructions are also called the Boolean operators. Note that in the Intel literature the TEST opcode is included in the logical instructions.

There are four logical instructions in the 80x86: AND, OR, XOR, and NOT. The action performed by these instructions corresponds exactly with the action of the fundamental operators of Boolean algebra. Therefore, in the 80x86 logical operations each bit in one operand is combined with the corresponding bit in the other operand, according to the truth table for the specific Boolean function. The operation is performed bit by bit and does not carry over to the neighboring bits. This explains why the 80x86 logicals are sometimes classified as *bitwise operations*. Table 4.2 lists the truth tables for the logical operations AND, OR, XOR, and NOT.

TABLE 4.2 TRUTH TABLES FOR THE LOGICAL OPERATIONS

AND			OR			XOR			NOT	
0 0	0		0 0	0		0 0	0		0	1
0 1	0		0 1	1		0 1	1		1	0
1 0	0		1 0	1		1 0	1			
1 1	1		1 1	1		1 1	0			

The AND Instruction

The AND instruction performs a Boolean AND of the operands. This determines that a bit in the result will be set only if the corresponding bits are set in both operands. The action corresponds to the AND truth table in Table 4.2. A frequent use of the AND opcode is to clear one or more bits without affecting the remaining ones. This is possible because ANDing with a zero bit always clears the result bit, and ANDing with a one bit preserves the original value of the first operand. The program LESSON4.ASM uses this action of the AND instruction to isolate 2 bits in a byte operand (see text reference # 4). In the following example we clear the 4 low-order bits of the first operand by ANDing with a mask in which these bits are 0:

```
                    HEX                    BINARY
                    57H               0101  0111B
        AND         F0H               1111  0000B
                   -------            ------------
                    50H               0101  0000B
```

The TEST instruction sets the processor flags as if an AND operation had been executed, but does not change the values of the operands.

The OR Instruction

The OR instruction performs the Boolean inclusive OR of the operands. This determines that a bit in the result will be set if at least one of the corresponding bits in the operands is set. The action of the inclusive OR corresponds to that in the truth table of Table 4.2. Because the inclusive OR sets a bit in the result if either or both bits in the operands are set, a frequent use for this operation is to set one or more bits in an operand. This property of the OR operation can be described by saying that ORing with a 1-bit always sets the result bit, whereas ORing with a 0-bit preserves the value of the other operand.

For example, to make sure that bits 6 and 7 of an operand are set we can OR it with a mask in which these bits are 1, as follows:

```
                    HEX                    BINARY
                    17H               0001  0111B
        OR          C0H               1100  0000B
                   -------            ------------
                    D7H               1101  0111B
```

Because bits 6 and 7 in the mask (C0H) are set, the OR operation guarantees that these bits will be set in the result independently of whatever value they have in the first operand.

The XOR Instruction

The XOR operation performs the Boolean exclusive OR (XOR) of the operands. This means that a bit in the result will be set if the corresponding bits in the operands have opposite values. If the bits have the same value (1 or 0) the result bit will be cleared. The action of the XOR instruction corresponds to that in the truth table of Table 4.2.

Note that XORing a value with itself will always generate a zero result because all bits will necessarily have the same value. Some programmers use this property of the XOR operation to clear an operand; for example, the instruction

```
XOR       AX,AX
```

will make the AX register equal zero.

On the other hand, XORing with a 1-bit inverts the value of the other operand because 0 XOR 1 is 1 and 1 XOR 1 is 0 (see Table 4.2). By properly selecting an XOR mask the programmer can control which bits of the operand are inverted and which are preserved. For example, to invert the two high-order bits of an operand you can XOR with a mask in which these bits are set. If the remaining bits are clear in the mask, the original value of these bits will be preserved in the result, as in the following example:

	HEX	BINARY
	55H	0101 0101B
XOR	C0H	1100 0000B
	----	-----------
	95H	1001 0101B

The NOT Instruction

The NOT instruction is the simplest of the 80x86 logicals. It acts on a single operand by inverting all its bits. In other words, the NOT operation converts all 1-bits to 0 and all 0-bits to 1. This action corresponds with the Boolean NOT function. The following example shows the result of a NOT operation:

	HEX	BINARY
	55H	0101 0101B
NOT	----	-----------
	AAH	1010 1010B

4.4 ELEMENTS OF THE PROGRAM LESSON4.ASM

One of the initialization operations performed by the BIOS program at power-on consists of examining the optional equipment installed in the system and recording the result of these tests in memory. More specifically, the optional equipment installed is recorded at the memory word located at physical address 00410H. The equipment data word is part of a larger area, named the BIOS data area, which starts at segment address 0040H. Figure 4.2 shows the data stored in the BIOS optional equipment data word.

The program LESSON4.ASM examines the low-order byte of the BIOS optional equipment data word and determines if a mathematical coprocessor chip is installed in the system and if the video hardware is color or monochrome (see text reference # 5). The code then displays the corresponding diagnostic messages (text reference # 6). We have left other equipment determinations as a programming exercise for the student.

Logical address = 0040:0010H

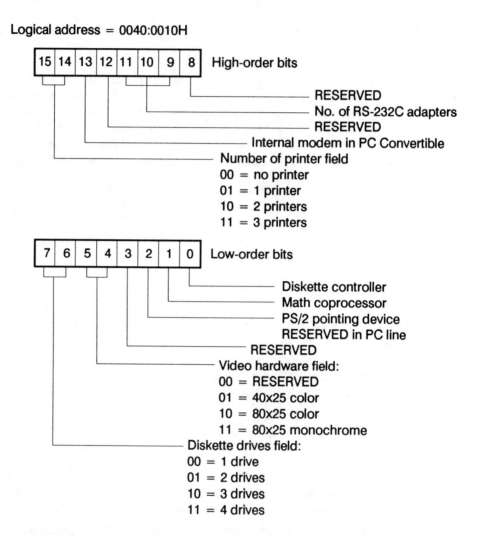

Figure 4.2 Optional Equipment Data in BIOS

The DISPLAY_MSG Procedure

The program LESSON4.ASM contains the procedure DISPLAY_MSG (see text reference # 1) that displays a formatted text string. The logic of the DISPLAY_MSG procedure can be seen in the flowchart of Figure 4.3.

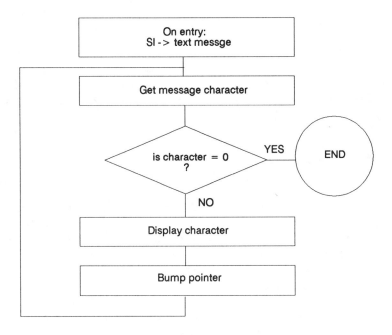

Figure 4.3 Flowchart for the DISPLAY_MSG Procedure

Compare Operation

In the program LESSON3.ASM we used TEST and JNE instructions to determine if a certain bit of the operand was set or clear. In the program LESSON4.ASM we use the CMP (compare) instruction followed by JNE (jump if not equal) to test for certain values of an operand. The compare instruction in text reference # 7 uses a decimal source operand, whereas in the instruction in reference # 8 the source operand is a binary number.

The actual operation of the CMP opcode is to set the processor flags as if the source operand has been subtracted from the destination. However, this subtraction is not actually performed since the values of the operands are not changed. Observe that the conditional jump instruction JNZ (jump if not zero) can also be coded JNE (jump if not equal). These are two different mnemonic words that correspond with the same operational code; in other words, the assembler program generates the same 80x86 instruction when encountering the JNZ or the JNE forms. Because the CMP operation performs a subtraction of the operands, the zero flag will be set if the operands are equal because the result of subtracting a number from itself will always be zero.

Incrementing a Pointer

The INC (increment) instruction is used in the DISPLAY_MSG procedure to bump the SI register pointer to the next character in the string (see text reference # 3). The INC instruction adds 1 to the current value of the operand, in this case the SI register. The reverse operation; that is, subtracting 1 from the operand is performed by the DEC (decrement) instruction.

Multiple Message Selection

The program LESSON4.ASM displays two of four possible messages according to the result of the test performed on the BIOS optional equipment data byte. Two of the messages refer to the mathematical coprocessor. The math coprocessor is an optional chip (designated as the 80x87) that can be installed in most IBM microcomputers to improve the precision and performance of mathematical calculations.

The program assumes that no coprocessor is installed and sets the SI register to point to a message stating this fact. If the test on the BIOS data confirms that there is no coprocessor, this message is displayed. If a coprocessor is detected, the message pointer is changed to another one that states that a coprocessor is present. This is a code-saving technique that can be used in various programming situations in which it is necessary to choose from two or more options. A little experimentation with this example will show that first performing the test and then selecting the corresponding message require more complicated coding than the method adopted.

Accessing Other Segments

Often a program will have to access other segments different from the assumed data, code, and stack. The ES (extra segment) register is often unassigned and can be conveniently used for this purpose. For example, the program LESSON4.ASM must access a data item located in the BIOS data area at segment address 0040H. Because ES is not used in the program, the code (see text reference # 9) sets it to the segment address in the conventional manner.

Once ES is set to the BIOS data area, it can be used to retrieve the byte at offset 0010H. However, because the program assumes that the DS register is used in accessing data, the code must override this assumption. The instruction used in LESSON4.ASM is coded as follows:

```
; Load byte into AL using segment override
        MOV     AL,ES:[0010H]    ; Offset portion using ES
```

Note that the segment override consists of the segment register name followed by a colon symbol. Also note that this override element is written outside of the indirection indicator (bracket symbols).

4.5 SOURCE CODE LISTING OF THE PROGRAM LESSON4.ASM

```
;******************************************************************
;******************************************************************
;                           LESSON4.ASM
;******************************************************************
;******************************************************************
; Program title: LESSON4
; Start date:
; Last modification:
;
; Program description:
; Display a screen message using a BIOS service
;
; New operations:
; 1. Display messages using BIOS service number 14, INT 10H
; 2. Read byte in BIOS data area
; 3. Test data byte for auxiliary equipment and display messages
;
;******************************************************************
;                           stack segment
;******************************************************************
STACK   SEGMENT stack
;
                DB      1024 DUP ('?')  ; Default stack is 1K
STACK   ENDS
;
;******************************************************************
;                           data segment
;******************************************************************
DATA    SEGMENT
;
PROG_MESSAGE    DB      'Program to identify optional equipment'
                DB      ' installed in the microcomputer'
                DB      0AH,0DH         ; New line
                DB      'by examining the BIOS data stored at'
                DB      ' address 00410H'
```

```
                      DB        0AH,0DH              ; New line
                      DB        0        ; Message terminator byte
; The following messages include the line-feed (0AH) and the
; carriage-return (0DH) codes to produce a new line and the
; message terminator code (0H)
MATH_YES          DB        'Math coprocessor present',0AH,0DH,0H
MATH_NO           DB        'No math coprocessor',0AH,0DH,0H
COLOR_VIDEO       DB        'Color video hardware',0AH,0DH,0H
MONO_VIDEO        DB        'Monochrome video hardware',0AH,0DH,0H
;
DATA     ENDS
;****************************************************************
;                           code segment
;****************************************************************
;
CODE     SEGMENT
         ASSUME   CS:CODE
;******************|
;  initialization  |
;******************|
ENTRY_POINT:
; Initialize the DATA segment so that the program can access the
; stored data items using the DS segment register
         MOV       AX,DATA              ; Address of DATA to AX
         MOV       DS,AX                ; and to DS
         ASSUME   DS:DATA               ; Assume directive so that
                                        ; the assembler defaults to DS
;*********************|
;    display first    |
;      message        |
;*********************|
; Set-up for pointer for display procedure
         LEA       SI,PROG_MESSAGE ; Set SI as pointer to message
         CALL      DISPLAY_MSG         ; Local display procedure
;*********************|
;  get BIOS data at   |
;     0040:0010H      |
;*********************|
;                                        |********************|
;                                        | text reference # 5 |
;                                        |********************|
; During system initialization the BIOS program stores the
```

```
; installed optional equipment at physical address 410H of the
; BIOS data area. This byte contains the following information:
; Bits  7  6  5  4  3  2  1  0
;       |  |  |  |  |  |  |  |____ Diskette controller
;       |  |  |  |  |  |  |_____ Math coprocessor
;       |  |  |  |  |  |_____ Mouse in PS/2 systems
;       |  |  |  |  |_____ RESERVED
;       |  |  |__|_____ 2-bit video hardware field:
;       |  |                       00 = RESERVED
;       |  |                       01 = 40 X 25 color system
;       |  |                       10 = 80 x 25 color system
;       |  |                       11 = Monochrome system
;       |__|_____ 2-bit diskette drive field
;                   00 = 1 diskette drive
;                   01 = 2 diskette drives
;                   10 = 3 diskette drives
;                   11 = 4 diskette drives
;                                    |*********************|
;                                    | text reference # 9  |
;                                    |*********************|
; First set ES to the segment element of the logical address
; 0040:0010H
        MOV     AX,0040H        ; Segment portion of address
        MOV     ES,AX           ; Segment to ES
; Load byte into AL using segment override
        MOV     AL,ES:[0010H]   ; Offset portion using ES
;
;*********************|
;   math coprocessor? |
;*********************|
; Assume that no coprocessor is installed and set message
; pointer
        LEA     SI,MATH_NO      ; Message is no coprocessor
; AL has equipment byte. Test math coprocessor bit
        TEST    AL,00000010B    ; Bit 1 is math coprocessor
        JZ      MATH_MESSAGE    ; Go if bit 1 clear
; At this point a math coprocessor chip has been detected
; Change message pointer
        LEA     SI,MATH_YES     ; Message is coprocessor present
;                                    |*********************|
;                                    | text reference # 6  |
;                                    |*********************|
```

```
MATH_MESSAGE:
; Display math coprocessor message
; Message pointer is already set
        PUSH    AX              ; Save equipment byte in stack
        CALL    DISPLAY_MSG     ; Local display procedure
        POP     AX              ; Restore equipment byte
;*********************|
;  video system color |
;    or monochrome?   |
;*********************|
; Assume that video system is color and set message pointer
        LEA     SI,COLOR_VIDEO  ; Message for color system
; Test bits 4 and 5 of AL to determine video hardware
; First step is isolating video system bit field
        MOV     AH,AL           ; Copy equipment byte in AH
;                                     |*********************|
;                                     | text reference # 4  |
;                                     |*********************|
        AND     AH,00110000B    ; Logical AND with mask
; AND operation clears all zero bits in mask. Only bits 4 and
; 5 are preserved
;                                     |*********************|
;                                     | text reference # 8  |
;                                     |*********************|
        CMP     AH,00110000B    ; Compare with pattern for
                                ; monochrome system
        JNE     VIDEO_MESSAGE   ; System is color
; At this point the system has monochrome video
; Replace video message
        LEA     SI,MONO_VIDEO   ; Message for monochrome
VIDEO_MESSAGE:
; Display video display message
; Message pointer is already set
        PUSH    AX              ; Save equipment byte in stack
        CALL    DISPLAY_MSG     ; Local display procedure
        POP     AX              ; Restore equipment byte
;*********************|
;  wait for keystroke |
;*********************|
END_DISPLAY:
; The program uses BIOS service number 0, INT 16H, to wait until
; a key is pressed. This service has no entry requirements
```

```
        MOV     AH,0            ; Service request number
        INT     16H             ; Transfer control to BIOS
; After the user presses any key the program ends by returning
; control to MS-DOS
;*******************|
;   exit to DOS     |
;*******************|
; After the message is displayed the program gives back control
; to MS DOS using service number 76
DOS_EXIT:
        MOV     AH,76           ; DOS service request code
        MOV     AL,0            ; No error code returned
        INT     21H             ; TO DOS
;*****************************************************************
;                         procedures
;*****************************************************************
DISPLAY_MSG     PROC    NEAR
;                                   |*******************|
;                                   | text reference # 1 |
;                                   |*******************|
; Display a message stored in the data segment using BIOS service
; number 14, INT 10H (BIOS teletype write)
; On entry:
;       SI — start of the message to be displayed
; On exit:
;       Nothing
; BIOS service requirements:
;       AH = service request number (14)
;       AL holds character to be displayed
;       BH = display page (normally 0)
;       BL = foreground color in the graphics mode (normally 0)
        MOV     BX,0            ; Display page and not graphics
                                ; mode
        MOV     AH,14           ; Service request number
DISPLAY_ONE:
;                                   |*******************|
;                                   | text reference # 2 |
;                                   |*******************|
        MOV     AL,[SI]         ; Message character to AL
;                                   |*******************|
;                                   | text reference # 7 |
;                                   |*******************|
```

```
        CMP     AL,0            ; Test for the terminator code
        JNE     DISPLAY_CHAR    ; Display character if not 0
; At this point the end of the message was reached
        RET
; At this point AL holds a character to be displayed
; The program saves the registers SI on the stack
DISPLAY_CHAR:
        PUSH    SI              ; Preserve message pointer
        INT     10H             ; Transfer control to BIOS
                                ; service number 14, INT 10H
        POP     SI              ; Restore registers
;                                       |********************|
;                                       | text reference # 3 |
;                                       |********************|
        INC     SI              ; Bump pointer to next character
        JMP     DISPLAY_ONE     ; Repeat processing
DISPLAY_MSG     ENDP
;****************************************************************
CODE    ENDS
        END     ENTRY_POINT     ; Reference to label at which
                                ; execution starts
```

VOCABULARY

addressing modes	logical instructions
base register	offset register
bitwise operations	operand address
direct addressing	physical address
effective address	register
index register	indirection indicators
segment register	segmented memory

QUESTIONS

1. How many registers are required in segmented memory addressing?
2. Express as a physical address the logical address B000:0010H.
3. Express as a logical address the physical address 410H
4. Is the instruction MOV DS,DATA a legal one?
5. What is the purpose of the ASSUME directive.
6. What addressing mode is used if the operand is a numeric value?

7. What addressing mode is used if the operand is the contents of a memory location specified by the SI register?
8. What symbols are used in indirect addressing and what are they called?
9. What logical operation is performed by the TEST instruction?
10. What is the difference between the OR and the XOR instructions?
11. What happens to the 1-bits after a NOT operation?

EXERCISES

1. Draw a flowchart of the program LESSON4.ASM.
2. Write a version of the program LESSON4.ASM in which the TEST instruction is not used.
3. Write a program that determines the presence of a diskette controller and the number of dirives in an IBM microcomputer system.

5

Video Hardware, Modes, and the System Cursor

5.0 VIDEO MODES

Programs for the IBM microcomputers are often classified in two general groups: alphanumeric or text programs and graphics programs. This classification is related to the two modes of operation of the video display hardware as described in the original listings of the IBM BIOS. Note that the concept of video modes is not used in OS/2 and other operating systems for the IBM microcomputers.

The alphanumeric modes are also called the text or alpha modes. In these modes the display function is limited to the characters in the IBM extended set (see Appendix C). While in the graphics modes, also known as all-points addressable, or APA, modes, the video system can control each individual screen dot, called a pixel.

The alphanumeric or text modes are dimensioned usually by the number of characters in each screen row and the number of rows displayed on the screen. In the graphics mode the screen surface is divided into a much finer grid of pixel rows and pixel columns. Both alphanumeric and graphics modes can be in color or in monochrome (black and white), according to the video hardware. Table 5.1 shows the principal characteristics of the IBM microcomputer video modes.

Because the text modes do not allow the control of the individual screen pixels, the programmer cannot display elaborate graphic figures in these modes. However, to compensate for this limitation, the IBM character set (see Appendix C) provides some special characters that allow limited drawing of boxes, solid figures, and shading screen areas. The program LESSON5.ASM at the end of this chapter displays the IBM extended character set on a frame created with some of these graphics characters.

TABLE 5.1 VIDEO DISPLAY MODES

MODE	TYPE	BW/ COLOR	NO. OF COLORS	GRAPHICS RESOLUTION	TEXT ELEMENTS	
					COLUMNS	ROWS
0	Text	BW	—	320 x 200	40	25
1	Text	Color	16	320 x 200	40	25
2	Text	BW	—	640 x 200	80	25
3	Text	Color	16	640 x 200	80	25
4	GRA	Color	4	320 x 200		
5	GRA	Color	2	320 x 200		
6	GRA	Color	2	640 x 200		
7	Text	BW	—	720 x 350	80	25
13	GRA	Color	16	320 x 200		
14	GRA	Color	4	640 x 200		
15	GRA	Color	2	640 x 350		
16	GRA	Color	16	640 x 350		
17	GRA	Color	2	640 x 480		
18	GRA	Color	16	640 x 480		
19	GRA	Color	256	320 x 200		

GRA = Graphics modes
BW = Black and white

Setting the Video Display Mode

Many simple programs in assembly language use the currently active video display mode. Many programs that perform text display functions assume that a text mode is presently active because the MS-DOS command prompt and program loader default to a text mode. For the same reason, a graphics program can rarely assume that the adequate graphics mode is already active.

In any case, a program about to change the video mode should first ascertain that the new mode is available in the video hardware. In text modes this operation can be simplified because monochrome systems can operate only in text mode number 7, whereas color systems use color text modes 1 and 3 or black and white text modes 0 and 2 (see Table 5.1). In the program LESSON5.ASM we can see that bits 4 and 5 of the BIOS auxiliary equipment byte encode the video display hardware installed in the system. If these two bits are set, then the system is a Monochrome Display Adapter (see Section 5.3) and the active video mode must be mode number 7. If not, any of the color text modes (0 to 3 in Table 5.1) can be used. The display mode is set using service number 0 of interrupt 10H.

5.1 THE SYSTEM CURSOR

Most computer systems use a small, flashing rectangle to mark the active position on the video display. This flashing symbol is called the *cursor*. In the IBM microcomputers the cursor is not a blinking screen character but a separate entity managed independently by the video hardware. BIOS provides several services to position and modify the system cursor. Service number 2 allows setting the cursor to any desired screen position. The procedure named SET_CURSOR (see text reference # 1) in the program LES-SON5.ASM sets the cursor to a row and column position using this BIOS service.

5.2 TEXT MODE ORGANIZATION

Text modes numbers 0 and 1 consist of 40 columns and 25 rows, whereas the remaining text modes consist of 80 columns by 25 rows (see Table 5.1). Because, in practice, the 40 x 25 modes are rarely used, screen routines that operate in the alphanumeric modes usually address a video screen composed of 80 columns and 25 rows.

Most video systems used in IBM and IBM-compatible microcomputers are *memory mapped*. The exception is the 8514-A display adapter, a very high resolution system that has gained little popular favor. To the assembly language programmer a memory-mapped video system appears as a region of memory associated with the video function in such a way that if a character is stored in this region it will automatically appear on the video screen. The mechanics by which this memory area is imaged on the video terminal is performed by the video hardware in a manner that is, for the most part, transparent to the software. In Chapter 7 we will develop display routines that access video memory directly, for which we will need detailed knowledge of video memory mapping. But even when we use the BIOS display services we need some understanding of video memory organization.

The most important characteristic of the structure of the IBM video systems in alphanumeric modes is that each character is displayed according to certain *attributes*. For example, in monochrome mode number 7, the display attributes are underline, bright, flashing, reverse video, and normal. Figure 5.1 shows the display attributes in monochrome and color systems.

The display characteristics can be determined from Figure 5.1 by comparing the bit setting of the attribute byte with the functions assgined to each bit and bit field. If a system is monochrome, the upper part of Figure 5.1 is applicable. If a system is color, the characteristics are determined from the lower bit map. For example, refering to Figure 5.1 we can see that the attribute encoding 00000111B (07H) corresponds to normal display in a monochrome system and to light grey characters on a black background in color systems. Note that the attribute value of 07H is usually considered as a normal attribute. The display attribute is used by several BIOS video display services.

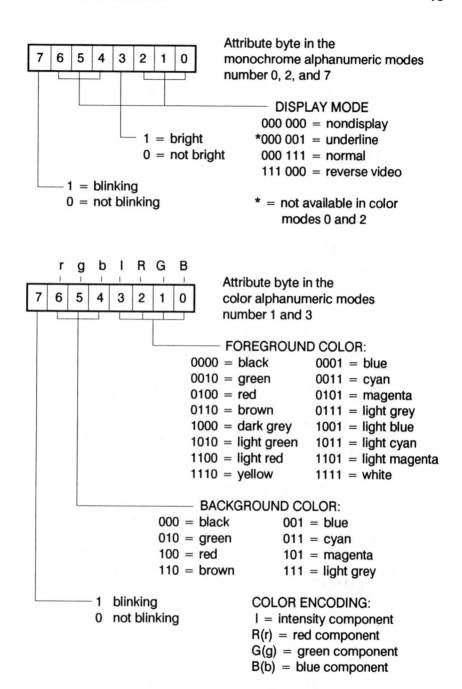

Figure 5.1 Attribute Byte in Monochrome and Color Modes

5.3 IBM VIDEO SYSTEMS

IBM video hardware has undergone many changes and modifications. The original microcomputers of the PC line offered several video options that could be selected by the buyer. The systems of the PS/2 line, on the other hand, come equipped with a standard video display, although there are some upgrade options.

The Monochrome Display Adapter

The *Monochrome Display Adapter* (MDA) is the original black-and-white display for the Personal Computer. This video system is furnished with an adapter card named Monochrome Display and Printer Adapter. A popular version of the MDA card, developed by Hercules Computer Technologies, is the *Hercules Graphics Card*. An advantage of the Hercules Graphics Card over the original MDA card is that the Hercules system can perform all the monochrome operations of the MDA and, in addition, can operate the display in a graphic mode. The MDA card and the Hercules Graphics Card are compatible with the IBM PC, PC XT, and PC AT. These monochrome systems can operate only in video mode number 7.

The Color-Graphics Adapter

At the time of the introduction of the original Personal Computer IBM unveiled a color graphics video system named the *Color-Graphics Adapter* (CGA). CGA was furnished as an optional adapter card and monitor. The system is compatible with the IBM PC, PC XT, and PC AT. It operates on video modes 0 to 6 (see Table 5.1). Of these, modes 0 to 3 are alphanumeric and modes 4 to 6 are graphics.

The Enhanced Graphics Adapter

The *Enhanced Graphics Adapter* (EGA) was introduced by IBM in 1985 at the same time as the PC AT. EGA is furnished as an optional adapter card and requires a special monitor. The system can emulate most of the functions of the MDA and the CGA but has much better definition than the CGA in the alphanumeric modes. An interesting feature of the EGA is that it can operate in monochrome alphanumeric mode number 7 as if it were a monochrome system. In addition, the EGA has four enhanced modes, numbered 13 to 16, that provide high-resolution graphics (see Table 5.1).

The PS/2 Multicolor Graphics Array

In the PS/2 line of IBM microcomputers the video hardware is furnished as an integral part of the system, in contrast with the video adapters of the PC line. The *Multicolor Graphics Array* (MCGA) video system was introduced with the original IBM PS/2 Model

30 and is also used in the PS/2 Model 25. In a way these machines constitute an exception because the original versions of the Model 25 and Model 30 are also compatible with the video cards used in the PC line. The MCGA emulates the CGA and can operate in all CGA modes. In addition, the MCGA has two high-resolution graphics modes, number 17 and number 19 in Table 5.1. The MCGA system became quickly outdated and was not used in later models of the PS/2 line.

The PS/2 Video Graphics Array

The *Video Graphics Array* (VGA) was introduced with the micro channel models of the PS/2 line, specifically the Model 50, 60, 70, and 80. VGA supports all the display modes of the MDA, CGA, EGA, MCGA, and, in addition, provides graphic mode number 18, with a 640 x 480 pixel resolution in 16 colors. In the newer machines of the PS/2 line the VGA system has replaced the MCGA system.

5.4 ELEMENTS OF THE PROGRAM LESSON5.ASM

The program LESSON5.ASM displays on the video screen a table of the IBM extended character set similar to the one in Appendix C. The characters, which include the normal ASCII set as well as the proprietary IBM extended set, are displayed on a graphics frame. This frame, which is divided into two areas, is drawn by using some of the box-drawing characters in the extended set. The outside margin of the frame lists the hexadecimal numbers that can be used as interception points to determine the value of each character.

Enhanced Display Routine

In the programs listed in previous chapters we used MS-DOS and BIOS services to display text messages encoded in a simple format that contained only a terminator code. In MS-DOS service number 9 of interrupt 21H (see in LESSON3.ASM) the message terminator code is the $. In Chapter 4 we developed a procedure (named DIS-PLAY_MSG) to display a message terminated in 0H using BIOS teletype service number 14 of interrupt 10H.

However, both of these services offer limited possibilities: the text message is displayed at the current cursor position, the message must consist of a single screen line, and no control is provided regarding display attributes. In the program LESSON5.ASM we develop a more sophisticated display procedure, named SHOW_BLOCK, that allows the display of a multiline message, with a certain attribute, located at any desired screen position (see text reference # 2). The logic used by the SHOW_BLOCK procedure is shown in the flowchart of Figure 5.2.

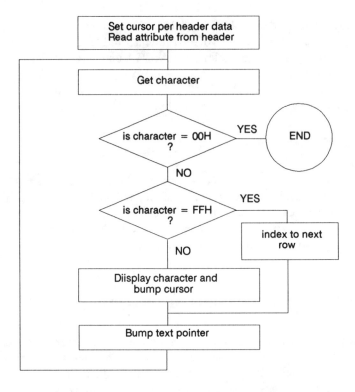

Figure 5.2 Flowchart for the SHOW_BLOCK Procedure

The characteristics of the display routine determine the format of the text message. The message CHARS_FRAME in the data segment of LESSON5.ASM (see text reference # 3) is structured according to this format. The display routine, in this case the procedure SHOW_BLOCK, expects to find the start row and column in offsets 0 and 1 of the message, the display attribute at offset 2, and the text message starting at offset 3. The control code 0H marks the end of the display block and must be the last character in the block. If the message contains more than one line, the new-line code FFH is used to mark the end of each display line.

Alphanumeric Graphics

The IBM extended character set (see Appendix C) includes a collection of special characters that can be used in drawing boxes, shading screen areas, and drawing graphics figures using various solid shapes. Alphanumeric programs can make use of these characters to display many attractive graphics shapes and figures and even to create logos and oversized text. Figure 5.3 shows how a simple graphics box can be drawn using the characters in the extended set.

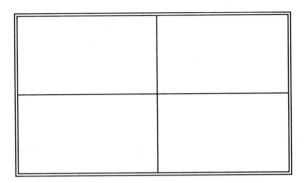

Characters used in box:

$\parallel$ = BAH $|$ = B3H $\dashv\!\!\!|$ = B6H

$=$ = CDH $-$ = C4H $\doteq$ = CFH

$\daleth$ = CBH $+$ = C5H $\top$ = D1H

Γ = C9H $\lrcorner$ = BCH

L = C8H $\vdash$ = C7H

Figure 5.3 Boxes Using Characters of the Extended Set

The text block named CHARS_FRAME in LESSON5.ASM (see text reference # 4) contains several graphics characters used in drawing the program's screen frame. The characters appear in each one of the 17 horizontal lines that form the frame.

Setting the Video Mode

It is generally a good programming practice not to assume that a certain video mode is active. A program can and should set the desired video mode, but first the code must make certain that the mode is compatible with the video hardware. The program LESSON5.ASM tests the BIOS auxiliary equipment byte, using a similar method to the one in LESSON4.ASM, to determine if the system is monochrome or color and sets the corresponding video mode using BIOS service number 0 of interrupt 10H (see text reference # 5).

Clearing the Video Display

Many programs require a clean video display on which to start their operations. Developing a routine to clear the video screen is therefore a useful function that can be reused. This can be performed in several ways. Perhaps the simplest one is to output to the screen 2000 blank characters (80 columns x 25 rows = 2000). A better option is to use BIOS service number 6 of interrupt 10H. This service performs two separate functions: the first one is to initialize a screen area to a certain character and attribute, and the second one to scroll the text lines in a window. In the following chapter we will use the scroll function of this service. The procedure named CLEAR_SCREEN in the program LESSON5.ASM (see text reference # 6) uses this BIOS service to clear the screen by initializing a window that includes all the screen area. The initialization values to clear the video display are a blank character and a normal attribute.

Displaying the Character Set

The core routine of the program LESSON5.ASM fills a graphics frame with the 255 characters of the IBM extended set. The characters are displayed in vertical columns of 16 characters each. The frame that holds the characters is divided into two areas. The left-hand area holds the characters in the range 0 to 7FH. These are the ones in the conventional ASCII set. The right-hand area holds the characters in the range 80H to FFH, which form the extended set.

The code uses the AL register to hold the character to be displayed. During processing the DH register holds the row address of the cursor and the DL register the column address. The routine's logic tests these values to determine the end of each column, the beginning of the right-hand area of the display frame, and the end of the processing (see text reference # 7).

5.5 SOURCE CODE LISTING OF THE PROGRAM LESSON5.ASM

```
;*****************************************************************
;*****************************************************************
;                          LESSON5.ASM
;*****************************************************************
;*****************************************************************
; Program title: LESSON5
; Start date:
; Last modification:
;
; Program description:
; Display a screen text block showing all the characters in the
```

```
;  IBM extended character set
;
;  New operations:
;     1. Set video mode
;     2. Clear the screen
;     3. Set the cursor at any desired screen position
;     4. Display a formatted block
;
;******************************************************************
;                            stack segment
;******************************************************************
STACK     SEGMENT stack
;
                  DB        1024 DUP ('?')  ; Default stack is 1K
STACK     ENDS
;******************************************************************
;                            data segment
;******************************************************************
DATA      SEGMENT
;                                           |********************|
;                                           | text reference # 3 |
;                                           |********************|
;  Message block formatted for the SHOW_BLOCK procedure
;  Header block format:
;          Offset:           Function:
;                  0 ---> Display row for start of message
;                  1 ---> Display column for start of message
;                  2 ---> Attribute for block
;  Embedded control codes:
;                  00H ---> End of message
;                  FFH ---> Index to next row
;
CHARS_FRAME       DB        1                 ; Start row
                  DB        12                ; Start column
                  DB        7                 ; Attribute
                  DB        '          IBM Character set'
                  DB        0FFH,0FFH
                  DB        '   0  1  2  3  4  5  6  7 '
                  DB        '   8  9  A  B  C  D  E  F',0FFH
;                                           |********************|
;                                           | text reference # 4 |
;                                           |********************|
```

```
          DB        ' ',0C9H,25 DUP (0CDH),0CBH
          DB        25 DUP (0CDH),0BBH,0FFH
          DB        '0 ',0BAH, 25 DUP (20H),0BAH
          DB        25 DUP (20H),0BAH,0FFH
          DB        '1 ',0BAH, 25 DUP (20H),0BAH
          DB        25 DUP (20H),0BAH,0FFH
          DB        '2 ',0BAH, 25 DUP (20H),0BAH
          DB        25 DUP (20H),0BAH,0FFH
          DB        '3 ',0BAH, 25 DUP (20H),0BAH
          DB        25 DUP (20H),0BAH,0FFH
          DB        '4 ',0BAH, 25 DUP (20H),0BAH
          DB        25 DUP (20H),0BAH,0FFH
          DB        '5 ',0BAH, 25 DUP (20H),0BAH
          DB        25 DUP (20H),0BAH,0FFH
          DB        '6 ',0BAH, 25 DUP (20H),0BAH
          DB        25 DUP (20H),0BAH,0FFH
          DB        '7 ',0BAH, 25 DUP (20H),0BAH
          DB        25 DUP (20H),0BAH,0FFH
          DB        '8 ',0BAH, 25 DUP (20H),0BAH
          DB        25 DUP (20H),0BAH,0FFH
          DB        '9 ',0BAH, 25 DUP (20H),0BAH
          DB        25 DUP (20H),0BAH,0FFH
          DB        'A ',0BAH, 25 DUP (20H),0BAH
          DB        25 DUP (20H),0BAH,0FFH
          DB        'B ',0BAH, 25 DUP (20H),0BAH
          DB        25 DUP (20H),0BAH,0FFH
          DB        'C ',0BAH, 25 DUP (20H),0BAH
          DB        25 DUP (20H),0BAH,0FFH
          DB        'D ',0BAH, 25 DUP (20H),0BAH
          DB        25 DUP (20H),0BAH,0FFH
          DB        'E ',0BAH, 25 DUP (20H),0BAH
          DB        25 DUP (20H),0BAH,0FFH
          DB        'F ',0BAH, 25 DUP (20H),0BAH
          DB        25 DUP (20H),0BAH,0FFH
          DB        ' ',0C8H,25 DUP (0CDH),0CAH
          DB        25 DUP (0CDH),0BCH,00H
;
DATA    ENDS
 ;***************************************************************
 ;                    code segment
 ;***************************************************************
 ;
```

```
CODE      SEGMENT
          ASSUME  CS:CODE
;**********************|
;     initialization   |
;**********************|
ENTRY_POINT:
; Initialize the DATA segment so the program can access the
; stored data items using the DS segment register
          MOV      AX,DATA           ; Address of DATA to AX
          MOV      DS,AX             ; and to DS
          ASSUME   DS:DATA           ; Assume directive so that
                                     ; the assembler defaults to DS
;                                    |**********************|
;                                    |  text reference # 5  |
;                                    |**********************|
;*********************|
;  test video hardware |
;*********************|
; First set ES to segment element of address
          MOV      AX,0040H          ; Segment portion of address
          MOV      ES,AX             ; Segment to ES
          MOV      BL,3              ; Assume color mode number 3
; Load byte into AL using segment override
          MOV      AL,ES:[0010H]     ; Offset portion using ES
; Test bits 4 and 5 of AL to determine video hardware
          MOV      AH,AL             ; Copy equipment byte in AH
          AND      AH,00110000B      ; Logical AND with mask
; AND operation clears all zero bits in mask. Only bits 4 and
; 5 are preserved
          CMP      AH,00110000B      ; Compare with pattern for
                                     ; monochrome system
          JNE      VIDEO_MODE        ; System is color
; At this point video hardware is monochrome. Set mode number 7
          MOV      BL,7              ; Change to monochrome mode
;*********************|
;   set video mode     |
;*********************|
; The video mode is set using BIOS service number 0 of interrupt
; 10H
VIDEO_MODE:
          MOV      AL,BL             ; Display mode to AL
```

```
        MOV     AH,0                ; Service request number
        INT     10H                 ; BIOS video interrupt
;*********************|
;  clear video display |
;*********************|
        CALL    CLEAR_SCREEN        ; Local procedure
;*********************|
;    display frame     |
;*********************|
; Characters of the IBM extended set are displayed on a graphics
; line frame that includes vertical and horizontal hex digits
; The frame is centrally divided into two areas. The area on the
; left holds the characters from 0H to 7FH. The area on the right
; holds the characters 80H to FFH
        LEA     SI,CHARS_FRAME      ; Pointer to graphics frame
        CALL    SHOW_BLOCK
;
;*********************|
;  display characters  |
;*********************|
;                                        |*********************|
;                                        | text reference # 7 |
;                                        |*********************|
; The 255 characters of the IBM extended set are displayed inside
; the graphics frame. AL holds the next character to be displayed
; DH and DL will hold the cursor address
; Begin by setting the cursor to start position inside frame and
; AL to the first character in the set
        MOV     DH,6                ; Row address for cursor
        MOV     DL,16               ; Column
        MOV     AL,1                ; First character to display
; Characters are displayed in vertical columns, 16 characters per
; column, starting at row number 5 and ending at row number 20
;*********************|
;  display one column  |
;*********************|
DO_COLUMN:
        CALL    SET_CURSOR          ; Local procedures to set cursor
        CALL    SHOW_CHR            ; and display one character
        INC     AL                  ; Next character to display
; Program tests AL for a value of 0FFH to determine if all
; characters in the extended set have been displayed
```

```
        CMP     AL,0FFH         ; Last character
        JE      EXIT_CHAR_SET   ; End routine if AL = FFH
        INC     DH              ; Bump counter to next row
        CMP     DH,21           ; Test for last row
        JE      NEXT_COLUMN     ; Go to next column
        JMP     DO_COLUMN       ; Continue along column
;*********************|
; index to next column |
;*********************|
NEXT_COLUMN:
        CMP     DL,37           ; Last column of first area
        JE      FRAME_AREA_2    ; Go to first character of second
                                ; area in frame
; Index to next column by adding 3 to the column counter
        ADD     DL,3            ; Distance between columns
        MOV     DH,5            ; Top row of next column
        JMP     DO_COLUMN       ; Column display routine
;*********************|
;  second frame area   |
;*********************|
FRAME_AREA_2:
        ADD     DL,6            ; Add six columns to counter
        MOV     DH,5            ; Row counter to first row
        JMP     DO_COLUMN       ; To column routine
;*********************|
;  end of display      |
;*********************|
EXIT_CHAR_SET:
; Set cursor at bottom of screen
        MOV     DH,22           ; Cursor row
        MOV     DL,0            ; Cursor column
        CALL    SET_CURSOR      ; Local procedure
;******************|
;  exit to DOS     |
;******************|
; After the message is displayed the program gives back control
; to MS-DOS using service number 76
DOS_EXIT:
        MOV     AH,76           ; DOS service request code
        MOV     AL,0            ; No error code returned
        INT     21H             ; TO MS-DOS
;
```

```
;*****************************************************************
;                           procedures
;*****************************************************************
;                                        |*********************|
;                                        | text reference # 6  |
;                                        |*********************|
CLEAR_SCREEN    PROC    NEAR
; Clear the video display using BIOS service number 6 of
; interrupt 10H
; On entry:
;           Nothing
        MOV     AH,06           ; Service request
        MOV     AL,0            ; Code to blank entire window
        MOV     BH,07           ; Normal attribute
        MOV     CX,0            ; Start at row 0, column 0
        MOV     DH,24           ; End at row 24
        MOV     DL,79           ; Column 79
        INT     10H             ; BIOS video service
        RET
CLEAR_SCREEN    ENDP
 ;*****************************************************************
;
;                                        |*********************|
;                                        | text reference # 1  |
;                                        |*********************|
SET_CURSOR      PROC    NEAR
; Procedure to set the system cursor using BIOS service number 2
; of interrupt 10H. The program assumes that a text mode is
; active and that the text screen contains 80 columns by 25 rows
; On entry:
;           DH = desired cursor row (range 0 to 79)
;           DL = desired cursor column (0 to 24)
; On exit:
;           System cursor positioned
;
        PUSH    AX              ; Save AX register
        MOV     BH,0            ; Display page 0
        MOV     AH,02           ; BIOS service request number
        INT     10H             ; Interrupt for BIOS service
        POP     AX              ; Restore AX
        RET
SET_CURSOR      ENDP
```

```
;****************************************************************
;
SHOW_BLOCK      PROC    NEAR
;                                       |********************|
;                                       | text reference # 2 |
;                                       |********************|
; Display a pre-formatted block message
; On entry:
;          SI -> start of block message
;
; Header block of formatted message:
;        Offset:          Function:
;                0 ---> Display row for start of message
;                1 ---> Display column for start of message
;                2 ---> Attribute for block
; Embedded codes:
;                00H ---> End of message
;                FFH ---> Index to next row
;
        MOV     DH,[SI]         ; Get row from header
        INC     SI              ; Point to start column byte
        MOV     DL,[SI]         ; Column
        MOV     CL,DL           ; Save start column in CL
        CALL    SET_CURSOR      ; Local procedure to set cursor
        INC     SI              ; Point to attribute byte
        MOV     BL,[SI]         ; Attribute to BL
        INC     SI              ; Bump pointer to message text
GET_AND_SHOW:
        MOV     AL,[SI]         ; Text character to AL
; Test for embedded controls codes
        CMP     AL,00H          ; Message terminator code
        JE      SHOW_END        ; Exit if terminator found
        CMP     AL,0FFH         ; Test for new-line code
        JE      LINE_END        ; Go to new line routine
; At this point AL holds a character to be displayed
        CALL    SHOW_CHR        ; Local procedure
        INC     DL              ; Next column
;
;********************|
;   bump cursor and  |
;   text pointer     |
;********************|
```

```
BUMP_PTRS:
        CALL    SET_CURSOR        ; Local procedure
        INC     SI                ; Bump message pointer
        JMP     GET_AND_SHOW
;**********************|
;    end-of-line       |
;**********************|
LINE_END:
        INC     DH                ; Bump row pointer
        MOV     DL,CL             ; Reset column to start column
        JMP     BUMP_PTRS         ; Prepare for next character
SHOW_END:
        RET
;
SHOW_BLOCK      ENDP
;****************************************************************
;
SHOW_CHR        PROC    NEAR
; Display character in AL, attribute in BL, at cursor
; On entry:
;           AL = character to be displayed
;           BL = display attribute for character
        PUSH    AX                ; Save general purpose registers
        PUSH    BX
        PUSH    CX
        PUSH    DX
        MOV     AH,9              ; Service request number
        MOV     BH,0              ; Display page
        MOV     CX,1              ; Repetition factor
        INT     10H
        POP     DX                ; Restore registers
        POP     CX
        POP     BX
        POP     AX
        RET
SHOW_CHR        ENDP
;****************************************************************
;
CODE    ENDS
        END     ENTRY_POINT       ; Reference to label at which
                                  ; execution starts
```

VOCABULARY

alphanumeric mode	memory mapped
attribute	micro channel
cursor	pixel
graphics mode	

QUESTIONS

1. What are the two general groups in which display modes are classified?
2. Can you control the individual screen pixels in an alphanumeric mode?
3. What BIOS service and interrupt can be used to set a video mode?
4. In which modes is it possible to control the individual screen pixels?
5. What is the system cursor?
6. How does a memory-mapped video system appear to the assembly language programmer?
7. What is the display attribute?
8. What is the code for a normal attribute?
9. What type of video adapter is the MDA?
10. What type of video adapter is the VGA?

EXERCISES

1. Write a flowchart for the display procedure starting at text reference # 7.
2. Write a version of the program LESSON5.ASM in which the IBM extended character set is displayed in two separate screens (as in Appendix D). Have the program wait for a keystroke before displaying the second screen.
3. Modify the SHOW_BLOCK display procedure so that an embedded control code (value 02H) will set the bright attribute bit (bit number 3) for the next character to be displayed.

6

Input, Output, and User Data

6.0 INPUT AND OUTPUT DEVICES

Input is the computer operation of processing incoming data so that they can be represented and stored electronically. *Output* is the operation by which data, stored electronically in the computer system, are translated into a form that can be understood by human beings. Computer input can take form using any means of communication that the device is equipped to process, for example, writing, speaking, drawing, and pointing. In the IBM microcomputers the classical input device is the keyboard. By the same token, output can take place using any communications media that can be interpreted by human beings, includeing written and spoken words, sounds, and drawings. The most commonly used output devices are the video display and the printer.

The Keyboard

The IBM microcomputer keyboard has undergone several changes regarding the number of keys, the presence or absence of certain control keys, and the repositioning of others. The number of keys has gone from 83 in the Personal Computer, 62 in the PCjr, 78 in the PC Convertible, and 84 in the AT, to 101 in the PS/2 keyboard. Some control keys have been repositioned several times; for example, the escape key (Esc) was located in the original Personal Computer keyboard at the extreme left-hand side of the top row, then moved to the right-hand side of this row in the AT, and back to the top left on the PS/2 keyboard. Most IBM keyboards are not interchangeable due to changes in the internal electronics and the connectors.

Each keyboard key is in fact a mechanical switch. The keyboard hardware detects each time that the user presses a key (switch closed) and each time that the user releases a key (switch open). The keyboard controller (which is a dedicated microchip) and the BIOS keyboard software calculate and store a specific code, called the *scan code*, for each key pressed and released. The action of pressing a key originates a *make scan code*, and the action of releasing the key originates a *break scan code*. Once the scan code is stored, the keyboard controller, using a mechanism called an *interrupt*, notifies the central processor that a key has been pressed or released. Hardware interrupts, such as the one generated by the keyboard controller, are discussed in Chapter 9.

Some keystrokes require immediate action, for example, the print screen, pause, or break keys. These keystrokes, called *hot keys*, are handled by BIOS routines that perform the corresponding action. Other keystrokes are used in interpreting previous or subsequent keystrokes, for example, the Shift, Alt, Ctrl, and Caps Lock keys. The keystrokes that are not hot, shift state, or control keys are stored in a BIOS memory area.

Keyboard Scan Codes

The internal scan codes stored by the BIOS keyboard handler are not represented in ASCII or any other standard format. Some BIOS services associated with the keyboard, available under interrupt 16H, return to the calling program both, the ASCII value of the keystroke, as well as the original make scan code. BIOS service number 0 of interrupt 16H, which waits for a user keystroke, returns the keystroke's ASCII code in the AL register and the original make scan code in AH.

In many cases a program can ignore the scan code and proceed according to the ASCII code returned by the BIOS service. However, on IBM microcomputers, many keys that are used in program operations, in manipulating the cursor, or in control functions do not have an assigned ASCII value. For example, regarding the function keys (labeled F1 to F10 in the PC line and F1 to F12 in the PS/2 line) BIOS service number 0 of interrupt 16H returns an ASCII value of zero in the AL register. For a program to determine which function key was pressed by the user it must examine the scan code, returned in the AH register. Table 6.1 lists the make scan code of some commonly used control keys.

Keyboard Programming

In LESSON3.ASM we used BIOS service number 0 of interrupt 16H to obtain a single keyboard character. This same service is used inside a program loop in LESSON6.ASM to obtain a series of keystrokes. We have mentioned that service number 0 waits for the user to generate a valid keystroke, then converts the scan code to ASCII and returns both values to the calling program. Some keystrokes are not directly returned by the service, for example, the Alt, Ctrl, and Shift keys.

TABLE 6.1 MAKE SCAN CODE FOR COMMONLY USED CONTROL KEYS

KEY	SCAN CODE	KEY	SCAN CODE
< Pg Up >	49H	< Home >	47H
< ⇑ >	48H	< ⇐ >	4BH
< ⇒ >	4DH	< ⇓ >	50H
< End >	4FH	< Pg Dn >	51H
< Ins >	52H	< Del >	53H
< F1 >	3BH	< F2 >	3CH
< F3 >	3DH	< F4 >	3EH
< F5 >	3FH	< F6 >	40H
< F7 >	41H	< F8 >	42H
< F9 >	43H	< F10 >	44H

Some control keys are conventionally associated with certain ASCII codes. In regard to these keys a program can act on the ASCII code, which is returned in the AL register. The program LESSON6.ASM, at the end of this chapter, identifies the Enter and Tab keys by means of their ASCII codes. Table 6.2 lists the ASCII codes associated with some control keys.

TABLE 6.2 SOME CONTROL KEYS ASSOCIATED WITH ASCII CODES

KEY	ASCII CODE	KEY	ASCII CODE
< Esc >	1BH	< Tab >	09H
< Enter >	0DH	< Backspace >	08H

Programs often need to determine if a key has been pressed by the user without suspending execution. BIOS service number 1 of interrupt 16H provides a keyboard scan function that sets the zero flag if no keystroke was produced. This service also includes a look-ahead function that reports the ASCII and scan code for the last keystroke in the same manner as service number 0. By using a combination of services number 0 and 1 it is possible to code a routine that will produce a *live keyboard* while the code is executing other functions. The following fragment shows the elements of this routine. The parts of the code that would be specific to the application are represented by ellipses.

```
; Processing routine for a live keyboard routine using BIOS
; service number 0 and 1 of interrupt 16H
;**********************|
;  test for keystroke  |
;**********************|
```

```
            MOV     AH,1            ; Service request number
            INT     16H             ; BIOS keyboard interrupt
            JZ      NO_KEY_PRESSED  ; Continue if no keystroke
;*********************|
;   get keystroke     |
;*********************|
; At this point a key was pressed. The code uses service number
; 0 to retrieve the keystroke
            MOV     AH,0            ; Service request number
            INT     16H             ; BIOS keyboard service
; At this point the ASCII code for the keystroke is in AL and
; the scan code in AH
            .
            .
            .
;*********************|
; continue execution  |
;*********************|
NO_KEY_PRESSED:
            .
            .
            .
```

We have mentioned that BIOS service number 1 of interrupt 16H also returns the keystroke codes in AX. But service number 1 does not remove the pending keystroke from the BIOS storage area. For this reason, the same keystroke will continue to be reported in successive calls to either service until it is removed by means of service number 0.

BIOS Keyboard Data

The keyboard service routine that is part of the BIOS program makes a record in memory of the state of those keys whose action is related to other keystrokes, such as the Shift, Ctrl, Alt, Caps Lock, Num Lock, Scroll Lock, and Ins keys. Figure 6.1 is a bit map of the BIOS data word at physical address 00417H.

A program that must determine if the user has pressed any of these keys must examine the BIOS data directly, as described in LESSON4.ASM, or use service number 2 of interrupt 16H. This BIOS service returns in the AL register the eight low-order bits at address 417H. Note that physical address 417H corresponds to the logical address 0040:0017H.

Logical address = 0040:0017H

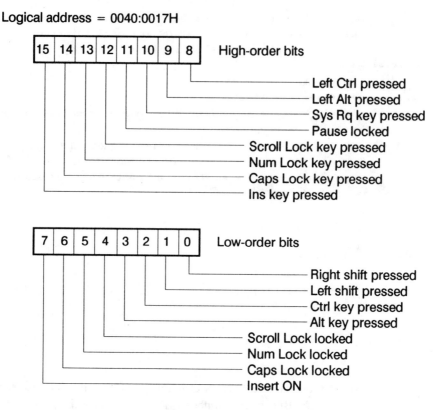

Figure 6.1 Keyboard Data in BIOS

6.1 THE PRINTER

After the video display, the printer is the most common and useful output device found on IBM microcomputers. Although it is considered an optional attachment, the printer is so useful that most installed systems are equipped with it. The printer provides a hard copy of computer data by making a paper record of the characters received through a communications connector.

In the IBM microcomputers, printers are usually connected to the system using a serial or parallel interface. In the *serial interface* data are transmitted bit after bit through a single line. In the *parallel interface,* by far the most common for printer operation, an independent line is provided for each bit to be transmitted. The parallel interface is so much associated with the printer that the system's *parallel port* is often referred to as the *printer port*.

There are considerable variations in the methods used by printing devices to produce a visible image on paper or other hard-copy media. If there is a mechanical collision between the printing element and the media, the printer is classified as an impact device. Ink jet and laser printers, on the other hand, are non-impact devices.

Printer Port Designations

Computer systems are often equipped with more than one printer. If so, there must be a way of identifying each printer device. In MS-DOS the printers are designated with the letters LPT (line printer) followed by single digit. Therefore, the first printer port is designated LPT1. The letters PRN (printer) are also used in MS-DOS to refer to the default printer, which normally coincides with LPT1. On the other hand, in BIOS the printer ports are designated starting with 0. The programmer must become familiar with these designations to avoid confusions and errors. Table 6.3 lists the MS-DOS and BIOS designations for three parallel ports

TABLE 6.3 DESIGNATIONS FOR THE PRINTER PORT

PRINTER NUMBER	DESIGNATION	
	BIOS	MS-DOS
1	0	LPT1 (PRN)
2	1	LPT2
3	2	LPT3

Printer Programming

Printer programming in the IBM microcomputers often consists of two steps: checking if the printer is ready to receive a character and sending the character to the device. In printer programming it is important to understand that, compared to the speed of the processor and other electronic components in the computer system, the printer is a very slow device. This means that a program can usually process characters much faster than they can be printed. If the printer status is not checked before a character is transmitted, it is likely that the program will overrun the device, resulting in lost characters.

BIOS provides several services associated with interrupt 17H that can be used in programming the printer. Service number 0 of interrupt 17H is used to send a character to any one of three printers. Service number 1 is used to initialize the printer port and service number 2 to obtain the printer status. Port initialization is normally performed by the system software; for this reason most applications ignore service number 1 of interrupt 17H. Because no harm results from reinitializing a printer port, this service can also be used to test if a port is available in a system, as shown later in this chapter. Another assumption made by most applications is that the printer addressed is the one connected to the first parallel port. Regarding the BIOS printer services, the first parallel port is numbered 0.

BIOS service number 0 of interrupt 17H transmits the character in the AL register to one of three parallel ports. If a printer is connected to the designated port, and if it is ready to receive, the character will be printed. All BIOS printer services require that the DX register be loaded with the printer port number. The valid range is 0, 1, or 2, but we have mentioned that in most cases it is safe to assume that the printer is connected to port number 0. All BIOS services return the printer status in the AH register. Figure 6.2 shows how the individual bits are used to reflect various conditions.

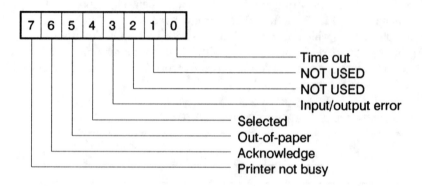

Figure 6.2 Printer Status Bits

The programmer must be careful in interpreting these bits because printers from different manufacturers report error conditions differently. In any case, bit 3 (input/output error) can be reliably used to determine if the printer is ready.

BIOS service number 1 of interrupt 17H initializes the printer port requested in the DX register. If a program is not certain that a particular port is available in the system, it can use this service to attempt to initialize it and then test the resulting status bits. If the initialized port is not reported as *selected* (see bit 4 in Figure 6.2), the code can assume that it is not available. The following fragment shows the required processing:

```
; Test to determine if the system contains a BIOS port number 1
; (LPT2)
        MOV     AH,1            ; Service request number
        MOV     DX,1            ; BIOS port number 1 (LPT2)
        INT     17H             ; BIOS printer interrupt
; The port status is in AH after initialization
        TEST    AH,00010000B    ; Test bit number 4
        JNZ     PORT_1_SELECTED ; Go if bit set
; At this point BIOS port number 1 is not available
        .
        .
        .

PORT_1_SELECTED:
; This label receives control if the system contains a BIOS
```

```
; port number 1 (LPT2)
      .
      .
      .
```

Printer Control Codes

All printers are designed to respond to certain control codes that activate nonprinting functions. Some laser printers respond to a complex control language with dozens of commands that include sophisticated graphics operations. Postscript and Hewlett-Packard's Printer Control Language (PCL) are two languages used in programming laser printers.

One of the problems of printer programming is that many of these control codes are not recognized by all devices. However, two printer control codes have gained almost universal acceptance: line feed (0AH) and carriage return (0DH). The line feed code, as its name indicates, moves the paper up one text line. The carriage return code resets the printing position at the start of the line.

The line feed and carriage return controls are recognized also by MS-DOS video service number 9 of interrupt 21H and by BIOS video service number 14 of interrupt 10H. We have embedded line feed and carriage return codes in the text messages listed in LESSON3.ASM, LESSON4.ASM, and LESSON5.ASM. In printer programming the software must usually sends to the device a line feed (0AH) and carriage return (0DH) at the end of each printed line.

6.2 STORING USER DATA

We have seen how a program can create and access data in its own memory space by means of data items associated with a variable name. In this manner we have used the DB (define bytes) assembler directive to store predefined text strings in the data segment. But often a program must store and access data that are not defined at assembly time; for example, an editor program must operate on the user's input so that the text can be redisplayed, edited, printed, saved to a disk file, or otherwise manipulated by the software.

In order to store data that are not defined at assembly time the program reserves memory space and assigns to this reserved area an identifying name. These reserved areas can be of any size allowed by the assembler. The IBM microcomputer assemblers allow the creation of data items according to the directives in Table 6.4.

TABLE 6.4 DATA DEFINITION ASSEMBLER DIRECTIVES

DIRECTIVE		NUMBER OF BYTES	DESCRIPTION
DB	define bytes	1	Allocates memory in byte-size units
DW	define words	2	Allocates memmory in word-size units
DD	define doubleword	4	Allocates memory in doubleword units. Used chiefly in numeric applications
DQ	define quadword	8	Allocates memory in quadruple word units. Used chiefly in numeric applications
DT	define tenbyte	10	Allocates memory in tenbyte units. Used chiefly in numeric applications

Assembler directives can be used to create one or more memory items of the same type. In previous programs we have used the single quote and comma symbols with the DB directive in order to mix ASCII text and numeric control codes (see also text reference # 1 in the program LESSON6.ASM).

When memory items are to be accessed using units different from those with which they were created, the assembler must be informed by means of a PTR operator. Consider a data item that was defined using the DW directive (word-size storage units) and the first byte in this item is to be loaded into a byte-size machine register. Or consider two byte-size data items that are to be loaded into a word-size register, as in the following example:

```
DATA      SEGMENT
WORD_ITEM        DW        01234H
BYTE_ITEM_1      DB        01H
                 DB        02H
DATA      ENDS
CODE      SEGMENT
          .
          .
          .
          MOV       AL,BYTE PTR WORD_ITEM
          MOV       AX,WORD PTR BYTE_ITEM_1
```

There is a PTR operator for each data definition directive, namely, BYTE PTR, WORD PTR, DWORD PTR, QWORD PTR, and TBYTE PTR.

Numeric data consisting of more than one item of the same size are sometimes called an *array*. If the multiple items are character data, they are often called a *string*. Reserved storage for multiple data items, of numeric or character type, is sometimes called a *buffer*. For instance, a typical editor program will create, name, and initialize a memory buffer to hold the user's text file. In the program LESSON6.ASM (see text reference # 2) we have created an 80-byte memory buffer that is used to hold the text in one screen line. Note that the DUP operator, which we have previously used in creating stack space, is used in this case to reserve a multibyte area in the data segment and initialize it to the value 0H.

6.3 ELEMENTS OF THE PROGRAM LESSON6.ASM

The program LESSON6.ASM listed in this chapter is a text editor with minimum functions. It allows the user to type text, one line at a time. When the user presses the < Enter > key at the end of each line, the program moves the screen line into a memory buffer area, adds the corresponding line feed and carriage return control codes, and sends the stored characters to a parallel printer. Note, in LESSON6.ASM, that the storing of screen text in a memory buffer is performed as a programming illustration because the program could easily have been designed to send the screen characters directly to the printer.

LESSON6.ASM takes advantage of the fact that BIOS service number 14 of interrupt 10H (the BIOS teletype service) recognizes certain control keystrokes. For example, the backspace key can be used in editing the characters already typed. After the line has been printed, the program sends a control code 07H, called a bell code, that will produce a beep on the system speaker (see text reference # 3).

Cascade Testing

The keystroke processing routine in LESSON6.ASM uses BIOS service number 0 of interrupt 16H to obtain a keystroke from the user. This keystroke is processed, in a cascade manner, by testing for each of the meaningful control codes recognized by the program. The < F1 > keystroke, used to end program execution, requires testing both the ASCII code and the make scan code reported (see text reference # 5) as described in Section 6.0. On the other hand, the Tab and Enter keys (see text reference # 6) are tested by their ASCII values.

Reading Screen Text

BIOS service number 8 of interrupt 10H provides means for reading a screen character and attribute into a machine register. Because service number 8 of interrupt 10H retrieves the character at the current cursor position, the program must first set the cursor to the desired screen location (see text reference # 7). Note that this routine stores the character in the buffer area reserved under the name LINE_BUFFER. The DI register is used as a pointer to the buffer area. The actual storage is performed by means of the instruction

```
        MOV      [DI],AL              ; DI -> buffer
```

listed in the code.

Scrolling a Screen Window

The program LESSON6.ASM uses BIOS service number 6 of interrupt 10H to scroll up a 20-line screen window. This scrolling of a limited screen area is done so that the program title and initial instructions are not erased from the screen as the text lines are moved up. The operation is shown in text reference # 8. Note that the CLEAR_SCREEN procedure in LESSON6.ASM uses another variation of this same BIOS service.

A Printing Routine

The procedure PRINT_ONE in LESSON6.ASM (see text reference # 10) is a simple routine for testing the printer for a ready status and transmitting a single character to the device if it is ready to receive. The routine uses the carry flag to report an error condition to the calling code. The calling routine tests the carry flag by means of a JNC (jump if no carry) instruction to determine if the character was successfully printed or if an error occurred (see text reference # 9). In case of an error an error message is displayed and program execution ends.

6.4 SOURCE CODE LISTING OF THE PROGRAM LESSON6.ASM

```
;****************************************************************
;****************************************************************
;                          LESSON6.ASM
;****************************************************************
;****************************************************************
; Program title: LESSON6
; Start date:
; Last modification:
;
; Program description:
; The program clears the screen and allows the user to type text
; at the bottom screen line. The code recognizes and executes the
; <Tab>, <Backspace>, and <Enter> keys. The <Enter> key sends the
; bottom screen line to the printer and scrolls the text up one
; line
;
```

```
; New operations:
;   1. Read the character typed by the user and process according
;      to the character code
;   2. Store text in a data buffer
;   3. Print characters
;   4. Scroll a screen window
;
;******************************************************************
;                          stack segment
;******************************************************************
STACK    SEGMENT stack
;
              DB       1024 DUP ('?')  ; Default stack is 1K
STACK    ENDS
;
;******************************************************************
;                          data segment
;******************************************************************
DATA     SEGMENT
;                                       |********************|
;                                       | text reference # 1 |
;                                       |********************|
TYPESIM_MSG      DB       '** A Typewriter Simulation Program **'
                 DB       0AH,0DH
                 DB       '   Press:',0AH,0DH
                 DB       '        <F1> key to end',0AH,0DH
                 DB       '        <Tab> for 10 spaces',0AH,0DH
                 DB       '        <Enter> to print line',0AH,0DH
                 DB       '$'
;
BAD_PRINTER      DB       '  *** PRINTER ERROR ***$'
;
;                                       |********************|
;                                       | text reference # 2 |
;                                       |********************|
; Buffer for text in one screen line
LINE_BUFFER      DB       80 DUP (0H)
;
DATA     ENDS
;******************************************************************
;                          code segment
;******************************************************************
```

```
;
CODE    SEGMENT
        ASSUME  CS:CODE
;**********************|
;    initialization    |
;**********************|
ENTRY_POINT:
; Initialize the DATA segment so that the program can access the
; stored data items using the DS segment register
        MOV     AX,DATA         ; Address of DATA to AX
        MOV     DS,AX           ; and to DS
        ASSUME  DS:DATA         ; Assume directive so that
                                ; the assembler defaults to DS
;
;**********************|
;  clear video display |
;**********************|
        CALL    CLEAR_SCREEN    ; Local procedure
;**********************|
;    set cursor at     |
;     screen top       |
;**********************|
; Cursor is positioned at the top of the screen to display the
; program's greeting and instructions message
        MOV     DH,0            ; Top screen row
        MOV     DL,0            ; Leftmost screen column
        CALL    SET_CURSOR      ; Local procedure
;**********************|
;    display greeting  |
;**********************|
; Display program entry message
        LEA     DX,TYPESIM_MSG  ; Pointer to message text
        CALL    DOS_DISPLAY     ; Local procedure
;**********************|
;    set cursor at     |
;    screen bottom     |
;**********************|
; Cursor is positioned at the bottom of the screen for program
; operation
        MOV     DH,24           ; Last screen row
        MOV     DL,0            ; Leftmost screen column
        CALL    SET_CURSOR      ; Local procedure
```

```
;                                      |*********************|
;                                      | text reference # 4 |
;                                      |*********************|
;*******************************|
;       cascade processing      |
;       of typed characters     |
;*******************************|
; Program monitors the keyboard for a keystroke and proceeds as
; follows:
;       KEY               ACTION
;       <F1>              End of execution
;       <Enter>           End of text line. Store screen line in
;                         buffer and send to printer
;       <Tab>             Move cursor right 10 spaces
;       others            Display character
;
GET_KEYSTROKE:
        MOV     AH,0            ; Service request
        INT     16H             ; for BIOS get key function
; Character is returned in AL and scan code in AH
;                                      |*********************|
;                                      | text reference # 5 |
;                                      |*********************|
        CMP     AX,3B00H        ; Test for <F1> key
        JE      DOS_EXIT        ; Exit if <F1> pressed
;                                      |*********************|
;                                      | text reference # 6 |
;                                      |*********************|
        CMP     AL,0DH          ; Test for <Enter> key
        JE      END_OF_LINE     ; Go to end-of-line routine
        CMP     AL,09H          ; Test for <Tab> key
        JE      TAB_ROUTINE     ; Go to tab key routine
; At this point there is a valid character in AL. Display
; character or execute control function using the BIOS teletype
; service
        CALL    TTY             ; Local procedure
        JMP     GET_KEYSTROKE   ; Get next keystroke
;*********************|
;    tab 10 spaces    |
;*********************|
TAB_ROUTINE:
        MOV     CX,10           ; Counter for spaces
```

```
TAB_10:
        MOV     AL,' '              ; Space character
        CALL    TTY                 ; Local procedure
        LOOP    TAB_10
        JMP     GET_KEYSTROKE       ; Monitor next keystroke
;*********************|
;   <Enter> pressed   |
;*********************|
END_OF_LINE:
        MOV     AL,14H              ; Paragraph mark to screen
        CALL    TTY                 ; Local procedure
;                                   |*********************|
;                                   |  text reference # 7 |
;                                   |*********************|
;*********************|
; move screen line to |
;       buffer        |
;*********************|
; Recover characters from the bottom screen line and store them
; in LINE_BUFFER. End routine at the paragraph symbol
; First reset cursor to start of bottom screen line
        MOV     DH,24               ; Last screen row
        MOV     DL,0                ; First column
        CALL    SET_CURSOR          ; Local procedure
; Set pointer to buffer
        LEA     DI,LINE_BUFFER      ; DI is destination pointer
; DX holds the cursor position during execution
; Get screen character at the current cursor position
GET_LINE:
        PUSH    DX                  ; Save cursor position
        PUSH    DI                  ; and buffer pointer
        MOV     AH,8                ; Service request number
        MOV     BH,0                ; Page 0
        INT     10H
        POP     DI                  ; Restore registers
        POP     DX
; Screen character is returned in AL
; Test for end of line
        CMP     AL,14H              ; Paragraph mark
        JE      IS_EOL              ; End routine on mark
; Not end of line, store character in buffer
        MOV     [DI],AL             ; DI -> buffer
```

```
            INC     DI                  ; Bump buffer pointer
            INC     DL                  ; Bump cursor column
            CALL    SET_CURSOR          ; Local procedure
            JMP     GET_LINE            ; Continue with next character
;*********************|
;     end-of-line     |
;*********************|
; Line feed and carriage return printer control characters must
; be sent to the device at the end of each line. These characters
; are now stored in the buffer
IS_EOL:
            MOV     AL,0DH              ; Line feed
            MOV     [DI],AL             ; DI -> buffer
            INC     DI                  ; Bump buffer pointer
            MOV     AL,0AH              ; Carriage return
            MOV     [DI],AL             ; Store in buffer
; The character 0AH marks the end of the text line at print time
;*********************|
;  print buffer line  |
;*********************|
; The characters stored in LINE_BUFFER are recovered and sent to
; the printer
            LEA     SI,LINE_BUFFER  ; SI is source pointer
GET_ONE:
            MOV     AL,[SI]             ; Buffer character to AL
            CALL    PRINT_ONE           ; Local procedure
;                                    |*********************|
;                                    | text reference # 9  |
;                                    |*********************|
; Test carry flag for printer error
            JNC     PRINTER_OK          ; Continue if no carry
;*********************|
;     printer error   |
;*********************|
; At this point a printer error has been detected. The program
; displays an error message and ends execution
            LEA     DX,BAD_PRINTER  ; Pointer to message text
            CALL    DOS_DISPLAY         ; Local procedure
            JMP     DOS_EXIT            ; Terminate execution
PRINTER_OK:
            INC     SI                  ; Bump buffer pointer
            CMP     AL,0AH              ; Test for end of text
```

```
        JNE     GET_ONE          ; Continue printing if not 0AH
;                                |*********************|
;                                | text reference # 3 |
;                                |*********************|
;*********************|
;      beep           |
;*********************|
; Use control code 07H to send beep sound to system speaker
        MOV     AL,07H           ; Bell control code
        CALL    TTY              ; Local procedure
;                                |*********************|
;                                | text reference # 8 |
;                                |*********************|
;*********************|
;    scroll screen    |
;*********************|
; Scroll the text window up 1 line from row 5, column 0 to row
; 24, column 79, using BIOS service number 6 of interrupt 10H
        MOV     AH,06            ; Service request
        MOV     AL,1             ; Code to scroll up 1 line
        MOV     BH,07            ; Use normal attribute
        MOV     CH,5             ; Start at row 5
        MOV     CL,0             ; Column 0
        MOV     DH,24            ; End at row 24
        MOV     DL,79            ; Column 79
        INT     10H
; Move cursor to start of line
        MOV     AL,0DH           ; Carriage return code
        CALL    TTY              ; Local procedure
        JMP     GET_KEYSTROKE
;******************|
;   exit to DOS    |
;******************|
; After the message is displayed the program gives back control
; to MS DOS using service number 76
DOS_EXIT:
        MOV     AH,76            ; DOS service request code
        MOV     AL,0             ; No error code returned
        INT     21H              ; TO DOS
;*******************************************************************
;                         procedures
;*******************************************************************
```

```
CLEAR_SCREEN    PROC     NEAR
; Clear the video display using BIOS service number 6 of
; interrupt 10H
; On entry:
;           Nothing
        MOV      AH,06           ; Service request
        MOV      AL,0            ; Code to blank entire window
        MOV      BH,07           ; Use normal attribute
        MOV      CX,0            ; Start at row 0, column 0
        MOV      DH,24           ; End at row 24
        MOV      DL,79           ; Column 79
        INT      10H             ; BIOS video service
        RET
CLEAR_SCREEN    ENDP
;****************************************************************
;
SET_CURSOR      PROC     NEAR
; Procedure to set the system cursor using BIOS service number 2
; of interrupt 10H. The program assumes that a text mode is
; active and that the text screen contains 80 columns by 25 rows
; On entry:
;           DH = desired cursor row (range 0 to 79)
;           DL = desired cursor column (0 to 24)
; On exit:
;           System cursor positioned
;
        MOV      BH,0            ; Display page 0
        MOV      AH,02           ; BIOS service request number
        INT      10H             ; Interrupt for BIOS service
        RET
SET_CURSOR      ENDP
;****************************************************************
;
TTY     PROC     NEAR
; Local procedure to display a character using BIOS teletype
; service number 14 of interrupt 10H
        PUSH     AX              ; Save AX in stack
        MOV      AH,14           ; Service request number
        MOV      BX,0            ; Display page is usually 0
        INT      10H             ; BIOS video service interrupt
        POP      AX              ; Restore AX from stack
        RET                      ; End of procedure
```

```
TTY         ENDP
;********************************************************************
;
DOS_DISPLAY       PROC       NEAR
; Display a formatted text string using DOS service number 9 of
; interrupt 21H
; On entry:
;           DX -> string terminated in $ sign
; On exit:
;           string is displayed at the current cursor position
        MOV       AH,9            ; Service request
        INT       21H             ; MS-DOS service interrupt
        RET
DOS_DISPLAY       ENDP
;********************************************************************
;                                    |********************|
;                                    | text reference # 10 |
;                                    |********************|
PRINT_ONE       PROC       NEAR
; Procedure to print one character using BIOS service number 0 of
; interrupt 17H. The code first makes sure that the printer is
; available and ready
; On entry:
;           AL = ASCII character to be printed
; On exit:
;           CARRY CLEAR indicates that the character was sent to
;           the printer
;           CARRY SET indicates that the printer was not connected,
;           off, not ready, or timed out
;
;********************|
;   test for ready   |
;********************|
; BIOS service number 2 of interrupt 17H is used to test if the
; printer is ready
        PUSH      AX              ; Save character and
        PUSH      SI              ; Buffer pointer
        MOV       AH,2            ; BIOS service request
        MOV       DX,0            ; Printer is number 0
        INT       17H             ; BIOS interrupt
; At this point bit 3 of the AH register is set if the printer
; is not ready
```

```
        TEST    AH,00001000B    ; Test status bit number 3
        JZ      SEND_CHR        ; Print character if bit clear
        POP     SI              ; Restore registers
        POP     AX
        STC                     ; Set carry flag to indicate
                                ; printer error
        RET
;**********************|
;    send character    |
;**********************|
SEND_CHR:
        MOV     AH,0            ; BIOS service request
        MOV     DX,0            ; Printer is number 0
        INT     17H             ; BIOS interrupt
        POP     SI              ; Restore registers
        POP     AX
        RET
PRINT_ONE       ENDP
;****************************************************************
CODE    ENDS
        END     ENTRY_POINT     ; Reference to label at which
                                ; execution starts
```

VOCABULARY

array   make scan code
break scan code   output
buffer   parallel interface
hot keys   scan code
input   serial interface
interrupt   string

QUESTIONS

1. Is the keyboard considered an input or an output device?
2. Are the IBM keyboards interchangeable?
3. What are the scan codes?
4. Which BIOS interrupt is related to keyboard services?
5. How can a program tell if the Shift key has been pressed?
6. Is the printer considered an input or an outpur device?
7. How are the printer ports designated in MS-DOS?

8. Which BIOS interrupt is related to printer services?
9. What is the code of the carriage return command?
10. What is the code of the line feed command?
11. What is the name of a data item consisting of more than one element?
12. What are buffers used for?

EXERCISES

1. Write a flowchart of the PRINT_ONE procedure in LESSON6.ASM.
2. Design a procedure to clear a window located anywhere on the video display.
3. Modify the LESSON6.ASM program so that it tabs 20 spaces when the < F2 > key is pressed. Reduce the scrolled window by one line. Update the program entry messages to reflect the new active keystroke.

7

Direct Video Access and 80x86 Arithmetic

7.0 MEMORY MAPPED VIDEO

Display operations in an IBM microcomputer can be performed using the system services provided by BIOS and MS-DOS or by accessing the display hardware directly. In the past, IBM and other equipment manufacturers often discouraged programmers and developers from using direct access methods by warning that these programs might not be compatible with future video systems. But the considerable better performance and display control of direct access methods often weighted more in developers' minds than the fear of eventual incompatibility. Therefore, many major software products developed during the 1980s for the IBM microcomputers used direct access techniques. This circumstance eventually forced the hardware manufacturers to preserve the addresses and hardware structures used by direct access methods.

Note that in IBM microcomputers the display operation is perfomed by storing character codes and display attributes in a dedicated memory area. Therefore, the actual debate is whether this access is performed directly by the programmer or through a system service in BIOS or MS-DOS. In order to perform these operations directly the program must be able to determine the address of the memory area that is mapped to the video display function. This special area is often called the *video buffer*, the *regen buffer*, or simply *video memory*. Once this address is known to the program, display functions become as simple as any other memory read or write operation.

Access to the Video Buffer

The first step in coding a direct access routine for video display operations is determining the base address of video memory. In an alphanumeric display the base element of this address is B000H for monochrome systems (mode number 7), and B800H for all color alphanumeric modes. A program can decide if a system is monochrome or color in several ways. One of them is to use BIOS service number 15 of interrupt 10H (see Appendix B). In LESSON4.ASM we developed an alternative method for determining the video hardware installed in a system by testing bits 4 and 5 of the BIOS optional equipment data byte at address 00410H. This same method is used in the program LESSON7.ASM at the end of this chapter.

Once the video system has been determined, the program can set the base address of the video buffer using the value B000H for monochrome displays and B800H for color displays. Because SS, CS, and DS are frequently used for other purposes, most programs that access video memory directly use the ES register to hold the base address of the buffer. The actual instructions for loading ES with the segment base are similar to those for any other segment register. For example, the following routine can be used to set ES to the base address of a monochrome system:

```
MOV     AX,0B000H      ; Segment address for monochrome
MOV     ES,AX          ; To the ES register
```

In this case an ASSUME statement is usually not desirable, because it is better to let the program continue to access its own data using DS, and enter a segment override prefix for the instructions that access the video buffer.

Structure of the Video Buffer

The video buffer in the alphanumeric modes of the IBM microcomputers contains two data bytes for each character displayed on the screen. The data byte located at even-numbered offsets holds the extended ASCII character code to be displayed (see Appendix D). The bytes located at odd-numbered offsets in the buffer will hold the attribute, as described in LESSON5.ASM and listed in Figure 5.1. Each attribute byte refers to the preceding character byte in the buffer, as shown in Figure 7.1.

Usual practice in programs that access the video buffer directly is to use one of the index registers (SI or DI) to hold the offset in the buffer. If the AL register is then loaded with the character to be displayed and AH with the attribute for that character, the instruction

```
MOV     WORD PTR ES:[DI],AX
```

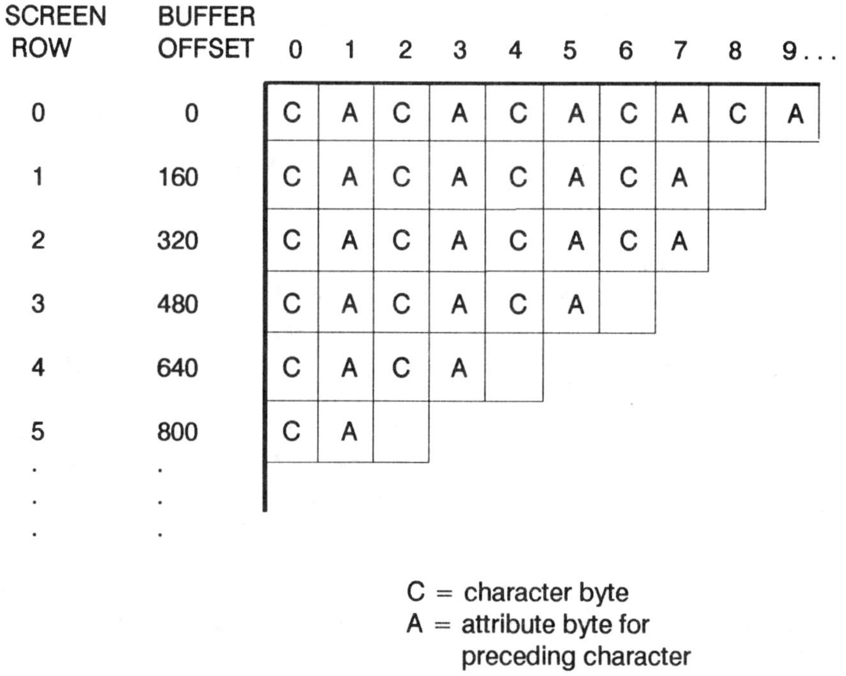

SCREEN ROW	BUFFER OFFSET	0	1	2	3	4	5	6	7	8	9...
0	0	C	A	C	A	C	A	C	A	C	A
1	160	C	A	C	A	C	A	C	A		
2	320	C	A	C	A	C	A	C	A		
3	480	C	A	C	A	C	A				
4	640	C	A	C	A						
5	800	C	A								
.	.										
.	.										
.	.										

C = character byte
A = attribute byte for
     preceding character

Figure 7.1 Video Buffer Organization

will place the contents of AL in the character position and the contents of AH in the attribute position according to the value of the pointer register (DI), which should always be an even-numbered offset. By the same token, in order to bump the pointer to the next character position in the buffer the code will have to increment the pointer register twice.

Use of the Cursor

One of the advantages of the system cursor is that some BIOS and MS-DOS display services provide automatic assistance in managing the cursor position. In LES-SON6.ASM we used BIOS service number 14 of interrupt 10H to display ASCII characters as well as to send the backspace control code to the video display. In this routine we were not concerned with the cursor position along the screen line, which was handled automatically by BIOS service number 14. But programs that access the video buffer directly have no such advantage. They must assume the management of the system cursor by updating its position whenever necessary, or they must disable the system cursor and use some other means of marking the current position on the video display.

Making the system cursor disappear from the screen is not a complicated matter. The video buffer area exceeds by 96 bytes the characters displayed on the screen (see Figure 7.2). This means that the cursor can be easily hidden by placing it in nondisplayed screen row number 25. This operation is shown in the following fragment:

```
; Hiding the system cursor by moving it to an undisplayed screen
; row
        MOV     DH,25           ; 26th screen row
        MOV     DL,0            ; First column
        MOV     AH,2            ; Service request number
        MOV     BH,0            ; Display page number 0
        INT     10H             ; BIOS video interrupt
;
```

It is possible to replace the system cursor with another screen object. Some programs use a rectangle such as the ones produced by the characters DBH to DFH of the extended set (see Appendix C). Graphics cursors offer many interesting programming possibilities, but it must be remembered that the system cursor, because it is not a screen character, can be displayed on the same screen position as the character that it marks. On the other hand, cursors created using character graphics will replace, on the screen, the character marked. This may be inconvenient in some text-editing operations.

7.1 IBM MICROCOMPUTER MATHEMATICS

Most general-purpose microprocessors, including the 80x86 family up to the 486, have limited power regarding mathematical calculations. Intel has compensated for this deficiency by means of a mathematical coprocessor chip that operates in parallel with the 80x86. But this mathematical device, named the 80x87 math coprocessor, is not furnished as standard equipment in most IBM microcomputers. This optional character of the math coprocessor chip has created considerable uncertainty for program developers. Finally, in 1989 Intel unveiled the 486 processor, which incorporates the mathematical functions, previously associated with the 80x87, in the main processor. The 486 is used in the XT line of IBM microcomputers, including the Model 90 and Model 95. Programming the mathematical coprocessor, or the mathematical functions of the 486 CPU, is a technical specialty and is not treated in this book. The student interested in this field will find several titles listed in the Bibliography. Our present concern regards the arithmetic instructions in the 80x86 and is limited to operations on integer numbers.

80x86 Arithmetic Instructions

The 80x86 microprocessors incorporate several instructions that can be used to perform simple arithmetic on signed and unsigned integers, on ASCII coded numbers, and on other numeric formats. It is possible to develop software routines that use these core operations to perform most mathematical calculations to practically any desired precision. But the development of this type of mathematical software programming is a specialty that exceeds the scope of this book.

The 80x86 arithmetic instructions can use 8- and 16-bit operands. The largest unsigned decimal number representable in 8 bits is 255 and in 16 bits is 65,535. Therefore (excluding the 80386 and 486), 80x86 arithmetic is limited to unsigned integers in a limited range. Nevertheless, as we have previously stated, this range can be extended to practically any limit by means of multidigit processing routines while the use of special numeric encodings allows representing signed and decimal operands.

Signed and Unsigned Representations

The 80x86 arithmetic instructions can operate on binary data. Some instructions can be used with either signed or unsigned operands. In 80x86 arithmetic a signed binary number is represented by encoding the number's sign in the most significant bit position. If this bit is set, the number is interpreted as negative. If this high-order bit is clear, the number is interpreted as positive. The use of the high-order bit to encode the sign of the number effectively reduces the representable range to one half of the integer values. Therefore, in signed representation, the range for a byte operand is reduced to +/- 127 and the range of a word operand to +/- 32,767.

Signed representations must be interpreted as such by the software, because there is no way to differentiate a signed from and unsigned encoding. For example:

		decimal value	
Hex	Binary	signed	unsigned
87H	10000111B	-7	135

The addition and subtraction instructions ADD (add), ADC (add with carry), SUB (subtract), and SBB (subtract with borrow) can be used with signed or unsigned integers. This is possible because the instructions update four status bits (flags) in a way that allows the results to be interpreted by the software as signed or unsigned. For example, the carry flag (CF) and the zero flag (ZF) are used in operations with unsigned integers.

The Intel mnemonics for multiplication and division instructions have been a source of confusion. The instructions IMUL and IDIV, which Intel refers to as *integer multiply* and *integer divide*, are used for operations with *signed* numbers, whereas the opcodes MUL (multiply) and DIV (divide) are used for unsigned operations. The association of IMUL and IDIV with the word *integer* seems to imply that there are instructions for *fractional* multiplication and division, which is not true. In any case, it is up to the software to interpret the result as signed or unsigned by evaluating the status flags.

Addition

The 80x86 ADD opcode performs the addition of two byte- or word-size operands, which may be signed or unsigned representations in byte or word size. The following code fragment illustrates the unsigned addition using an immediate and a register operand.

```
; Add 8 to the value in the AL register
        ADD     AL,8            ; Immediate addressing mode
        JC      AL_TOO_BIG      ; Go if sum exceeds the
                                ; capacity of AL (255)
; Add AX and BX
        ADD     AX,BX           ; AX = AX + BX
        JC      AX_TOO_BIG      ; Go if sum exceeds the
                                ; capacity of AX (65,535)
```

Subtraction

The 80x86 SUB opcode subtracts the source operand from the destination. The difference is placed in the destination operand. The operands may be byte- or word-size signed or unsigned numbers, for example:

```
; Subtract 12 from the value in CL
        SUB     CL,12           ; CL = CL - 12
        JC      BORROW_OUT      ; Go if CL > 12
```

Multiplication

The 80x86 MUL instruction multiplies the source operand by AL or AX register. Both operands must be unsigned binary integers. If the source operand is a byte, then it is multiplied by AL and the word product is stored in AX. If the source operand is a word, then it is multiplied by AX and the doubleword product is stored in DX and AX. For example:

```
; Multiplication of two byte-size operands
        MOV     AL,20           ; One factor to AL
        MOV     CL,50           ; Second factor to CL
        MUL     CL              ; AX = AL * CL
; Note that byte multiplication will never exceed a word result
; Multiplication of two word-size operands
        MOV     AX,20000        ; One factor to AX
        MOV     CX,50000        ; Second factor to CX
        MUL     CX              ; DX:AX = AX * CX
```

```
; Note that word multiplication will never exceed a doubleword
; result
```

In the case of word multiplication the product is found in two registers: DX and AX. In the above example the four high-order hexadecimal digits of this product (3B9AH) will be in DX and the four low-order digits (CA00H) in AX. Note that 1,000,000,000 decimal = 3B9ACA00H.

Division

The 80x86 DIV instructions divides AX or DX:AX by the source operand. Both operands must be unsigned binary integers. If the source is a byte, then the operation performed is AX / source. The quotient is returned in AL and the remainder in AH. If the source is a word, then the operation is DX:AX / source. In this case the quotient is returned in AX and the remainder in AX. For example:

```
; Division of word operand by a byte source
        MOV     AX,620          ; Dividend to AX
        MOV     CL,8            ; Divisor to CL
        DIV     CL              ; 620 / 8 = 77 quotient and a
                                ; remainder of 4
; AL will hold quotient (77) and AH the remainder (4)
; Division of a doubleword operand by a word source
; as follows: 800,425 / 32,000
; 800,425 = C36A9H
        MOV     DX,000CH        ; High-order word of dividend
        MOV     AX,36A9H        ; Low-order word of dividend
        MOV     CX,32000        ; Divisor to CX
        DIV     CX              ; 800,425 / 32,000
; Quotient = 25 (in AX)
; Remainder = 425 (in DX)
```

7.2 ELEMENTS OF THE PROGRAM LESSON7.ASM

The program LESSON7.ASM performs an almost identical operation to the program LESSON5.ASM. This consist of displaying a frame containing all the characters in the IBM extended character set (see Appendix C). The difference between these programs is that LESSON7.ASM performs this operation using direct access to the video buffer.

Setting ES to the Video Buffer Base

The code uses the ES segment register to hold the base address of the video buffer. Because alphanumeric operations use two different buffer bases, B000H if the system is monochrome and B800H if it is color, the code loads the DX register with the corresponding base address. The correct value is determined at the time that the program tests the video system hardware to set the display mode (see text references # 1). This buffer address, which is held temporarily in the DX register, is later loaded into ES.

Clearing the Screen

The procedure named CLEAR_DIRECT (see text reference # 2) clears the entire screen using direct access to the video buffer. A blank character (20H) is loaded into AL and the normal attribute code (07H) into AH. The DI register, which is used as an offset pointer into the buffer, is initialized to the first byte in the buffer by loading it with a value of 0H. The code assumes that ES has been previously set to the base address of the buffer and that the display is an 80-column x 25-row alphanumeric mode. The actual display operation is a memory write using the ES as a segment override, as follows:

```
MOV     ES:[DI],AX      ; Store character and attribute
INC     DI              ; Bump buffer pointer
INC     DI              ; twice to skip attribute
```

Using a Pointer Register

Direct access operations are performed independently of the system cursor. We have seen in the CLEAR_DIRECT procedure that the DI register holds the current offset into the buffer. This means that the value in DI determines the screen position that is being accessed. In other words, the DI register serves as a virtual cursor for the display routine. Assuming that the selected alphanumeric mode is one with 80 screen columns x 25 screen rows, the video buffer can be visualized as shown in Figure 7.2.

Using the screen row and column coordinates, the procedure named SET_DI (see text reference # 3) calculates the offset in the buffer for an 80 x 25 alphanumeric mode. The operations require integer multiplication by the number of bytes per buffer row (in this case 160) and integer addition of twice the column coordinate. These operations can be seen in the SET_DI procedure.

Displaying a Formatted Message

The procedure named SHOW_DIRECT (see text reference # 4) uses the same logic and message format as the procedure SHOW_BLOCK explained in Chapter 4. One difference between these procedures is in the handling of the current display position, which is determined by the location of the system cursor in SHOW_BLOCK and by the value in the DI register in SHOW_DIRECT. A second difference is in the actual display operation, which is performed by a BIOS service in SHOW_BLOCK and by a direct buffer access in SHOW_DIRECT.

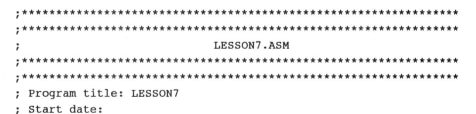

Buffer start:
Monochrome = B000H
Color = B800H

c = Character display position (even bytes)
a = Attribute display position (odd bytes)

Figure 7.2 Video Buffer in Alphanumeric 80 by 25 Modes

7.3 SOURCE CODE LISTING OF THE PROGRAM LESSON7.ASM

```
;****************************************************************
;****************************************************************
;                          LESSON7.ASM
;****************************************************************
;****************************************************************
; Program title: LESSON7
; Start date:
```

```
; Last modification:
;
; Program description:
; Display a screen text block showing all the characters in the
; IBM extended character set using direct access to the video
; buffer
;
;
; New operations:
;    1. Set the ES register to the video buffer base address
;    2. Clear the screen using direct access
;    3. Use of a pointer register for direct access operations
;    4. Display a formatted message using direct screen access
;
;*****************************************************************
;                          stack segment
;*****************************************************************
STACK   SEGMENT stack
;
                DB        1024 DUP ('?')  ; Default stack is 1K
STACK   ENDS
;
;*****************************************************************
;                          data segment
;*****************************************************************
DATA    SEGMENT
;
; Message block formatted for the SHOW_BLOCK procedure
; Header block format:
;       Offset:           Function:
;                0 ---> Display row for start of message
;                1 ---> Display column for start of message
;                2 ---> Attribute for block
; Embedded control codes:
;                00H ---> End of message
;                FFH ---> Index to next row
;
CHARS_FRAME     DB        1                 ; Start row
                DB        12                ; Start column
                DB        7                 ; Attribute
                DB        '       IBM Character set'
                DB        0FFH,0FFH
```

```
            DB          '   0   1   2   3   4   5   6   7 '
            DB          '   8   9   A   B   C   D   E   F',0FFH
            DB          '  ',0C9H,25 DUP (0CDH),0CBH
            DB          25 DUP (0CDH),0BBH,0FFH
            DB          '0 ',0BAH, 25 DUP (20H),0BAH
            DB          25 DUP (20H),0BAH,0FFH
            DB          '1 ',0BAH, 25 DUP (20H),0BAH
            DB          25 DUP (20H),0BAH,0FFH
            DB          '2 ',0BAH, 25 DUP (20H),0BAH
            DB          25 DUP (20H),0BAH,0FFH
            DB          '3 ',0BAH, 25 DUP (20H),0BAH
            DB          25 DUP (20H),0BAH,0FFH
            DB          '4 ',0BAH, 25 DUP (20H),0BAH
            DB          25 DUP (20H),0BAH,0FFH
            DB          '5 ',0BAH, 25 DUP (20H),0BAH
            DB          25 DUP (20H),0BAH,0FFH
            DB          '6 ',0BAH, 25 DUP (20H),0BAH
            DB          25 DUP (20H),0BAH,0FFH
            DB          '7 ',0BAH, 25 DUP (20H),0BAH
            DB          25 DUP (20H),0BAH,0FFH
            DB          '8 ',0BAH, 25 DUP (20H),0BAH
            DB          25 DUP (20H),0BAH,0FFH
            DB          '9 ',0BAH, 25 DUP (20H),0BAH
            DB          25 DUP (20H),0BAH,0FFH
            DB          'A ',0BAH, 25 DUP (20H),0BAH
            DB          25 DUP (20H),0BAH,0FFH
            DB          'B ',0BAH, 25 DUP (20H),0BAH
            DB          25 DUP (20H),0BAH,0FFH
            DB          'C ',0BAH, 25 DUP (20H),0BAH
            DB          25 DUP (20H),0BAH,0FFH
            DB          'D ',0BAH, 25 DUP (20H),0BAH
            DB          25 DUP (20H),0BAH,0FFH
            DB          'E ',0BAH, 25 DUP (20H),0BAH
            DB          25 DUP (20H),0BAH,0FFH
            DB          'F ',0BAH, 25 DUP (20H),0BAH
            DB          25 DUP (20H),0BAH,0FFH
            DB          '  ',0C8H,25 DUP (0CDH),0CAH
            DB          25 DUP (0CDH),0BCH,0H
DATA    ENDS
;****************************************************************
;                    code segment
;****************************************************************
```

```
;
CODE      SEGMENT
          ASSUME   CS:CODE
;*********************|
;    initialization   |
;*********************|
ENTRY_POINT:
; Initialize the DATA segment so that the program can access the
; stored data items using the DS segment register
          MOV      AX,DATA           ; Address of DATA to AX
          MOV      DS,AX             ; and to DS
          ASSUME   DS:DATA           ; Assume directive so that
                                     ; the assembler defaults to DS

;*********************|
;   test video hardware |
;*********************|
; First set ES to segment element of address
          MOV      AX,0040H          ; Segment portion of address
          MOV      ES,AX             ; Segment to ES
          MOV      BL,3              ; Assume color mode number 3
;                                      |********************|
;                                      | text reference # 1 |
;                                      |********************|
          MOV      DX,0B800H         ; Base address of color video
; Load byte into AL using segment override
          MOV      AL,ES:[0010H]     ; Offset portion using ES
; Test bits 4 and 5 of AL to determine video hardware
          MOV      AH,AL             ; Copy equipment byte in AH
          AND      AH,00110000B      ; Logical AND with mask
; AND operation clears all zero bits in mask. Only bits 4 and
; 5 are preserved
          CMP      AH,00110000B      ; Compare with pattern for
                                     ; monochrome system
          JNE      VIDEO_MODE        ; System is color
; At this point video hardware is monochrome. Set mode number 7
          MOV      BL,7              ; Change to monochrome mode
;                                      |********************|
;                                      | text reference # 1 |
;                                      |********************|
          MOV      DX,0B000H         ; Base address of monochrome
                                     ; video
```

```
;**********************|
;   set video mode     |
;**********************|
VIDEO_MODE:
        PUSH    DX              ; Save video base address
        MOV     AL,BL           ; Display mode to AL
        MOV     AH,0            ; Service request number
        INT     10H             ; BIOS video interrupt
        POP     DX              ; Restore base address
;                               |**********************|
;                               | text reference # 1   |
;                               |**********************|
;**********************|
;  ES to video buffer  |
;     base address      |
;**********************|
        MOV     ES,DX           ; Load ES with video base address
;**********************|
;  clear video display |
;**********************|
        CALL    CLEAR_DIRECT    ; Local procedure
;**********************|
;    display frame     |
;**********************|
; Characters of the IBM extended set are displayed on a graphics
; line frame that includes vertical and horizontal hex digits
; The frame is centrally divided into two areas. The area on the
; left holds the characters from 0H to 7FH. The area on the right
; holds the characters 80H to FFH
        LEA     SI,CHARS_FRAME  ; Pointer to graphics frame
        CALL    SHOW_DIRECT     ; Local procedure
;**********************|
;  display characters  |
;**********************|
; The 255 characters of the IBM extended set are displayed inside
; the graphics frame. AL holds the next character to be displayed
; First set cursor to first position inside frame
        MOV     DH,6            ; Row address for cursor
        MOV     DL,16           ; Column
        MOV     AL,1            ; First character to display
; Characters are displayed in vertical columns, 16 characters per
; column, starting at row number 5 and ending at row number 20
```

```
;*********************|
;   display one column |
;*********************|
DO_COLUMN:
        CALL    SET_DI              ; Local procedures to set cursor
; Display it by storing character in video buffer
        MOV     BYTE PTR ES:[DI],AL     ; Store character
        INC     AL                  ; Next character to display
; Program tests AL for a value of 0FFH to determine if all
; characters in the extended set have been displayed
        CMP     AL,0FFH             ; Last character
        JE      RESET_AND_EXIT      ; End routine if AL = FFH
        INC     DH                  ; Bump counter to next row
        CMP     DH,21               ; Test for last row
        JE      NEXT_COLUMN         ; Go to next column
        JMP     DO_COLUMN           ; Continue along column
;*********************|
; index to next column |
;*********************|
NEXT_COLUMN:
        CMP     DL,37               ; Last column of first area
        JE      FRAME_AREA_2        ; Go to first character of second
                                    ; area in frame
; Index to next column by adding 3 to the column counter
        ADD     DL,3                ; Distance between columns
        MOV     DH,5                ; Top row of next column
        JMP     DO_COLUMN           ; Column display routine
;*********************|
;   second frame area  |
;*********************|
FRAME_AREA_2:
        ADD     DL,6                ; Add six columns to counter
        MOV     DH,5                ; Row counter to first row
        JMP     DO_COLUMN           ; To column routine
;*********************|
;    exit routine      |
;*********************|
RESET_AND_EXIT:
; Set system cursor at bottom of screen using BIOS service
; number 2 of interrupt 10H
        MOV     BH,0                ; Display page 0
        MOV     AH,2                ; Service request number
```

```
        MOV     DH,23           ; Cursor row
        MOV     DL,0            ; Cursor column
        INT     10H             ; BIOS video interrupt
;******************|
;   exit to DOS    |
;******************|
; After the message is displayed the program gives control back
; to MS-DOS using service number 76
DOS_EXIT:
        MOV     AH,76           ; DOS service request code
        MOV     AL,0            ; No error code returned
        INT     21H             ; TO MS-DOS
;
;*****************************************************************
;                        procedures
;*****************************************************************
;                              |********************|
;                              | text reference # 2 |
;                              |********************|
CLEAR_DIRECT    PROC    NEAR
; Clear the video display using direct access to the video
; buffer
; On entry:
;         ES -> video buffer base address
        PUSH    AX              ; Save entry registers
        PUSH    CX
        PUSH    DI
        MOV     DI,0            ; Start at offset 0 in buffer
        MOV     AL,20H          ; Blank character
        MOV     AH,7            ; Normal display attribute
        MOV     CX,2000         ; Repeat 2000 times
CLEAR_2000:
        MOV     ES:[DI],AX      ; Store character and attribute
        INC     DI              ; Bump buffer pointer
        INC     DI              ; twice to skip attribute
        LOOP    CLEAR_2000
        POP     DI
        POP     CX
        POP     AX              ; Restore entry registers
        RET
CLEAR_DIRECT    ENDP
```

```
;****************************************************************
;                                        |*********************|
;                                        | text reference # 3 |
;                                        |*********************|
SET_DI          PROC    NEAR
; Set DI to the offset address in the video buffer that
; corresponds with a screen position expressed in terms of a row
; and column
; On entry:
;          DH = screen row (0 to 24)
;          DL = screen column (0 to 79)
;
        PUSH    AX              ; Save accumulator
        PUSH    DX              ; and DX
        MOV     AL,160          ; Bytes per row
        MUL     DH              ; AX = 160 * DH
        MOV     DI,AX           ; Save partial result in DI
        MOV     AL,2            ; Bytes per column
        MUL     DL              ; AX = DL * 2
        ADD     DI,AX           ; Add in previous result
        POP     DX              ; Restore DX
        POP     AX              ; And accumulator
        RET
SET_DI          ENDP
;****************************************************************
;                                        |*********************|
;                                        | text reference # 4 |
;                                        |*********************|
SHOW_DIRECT     PROC    NEAR
; Display a pre-formatted block message using direct access to
; the video buffer
; On entry:
;          SI -> start of block message
; Message format:
;       Offset:            Function:
;            0 —— Display row for start of message
;            1 —— Display column for start of message
;            2 —— Attribute for block
; Embedded codes:
;            00H = End of message
;            FFH = End of row
;
```

```
            PUSH    AX                  ; Save entry registers
            PUSH    CX
            PUSH    DX
            MOV     DH,[SI]             ; Get row
            INC     SI                  ; Point to start column byte
            MOV     DL,[SI]             ; Column
            MOV     CL,DL               ; Save start column in CL
            CALL    SET_DI              ; Set DI to offset in buffer
            INC     SI                  ; Point to attribute byte
            MOV     AH,[SI]             ; To AH
            INC     SI
GET_AND_SHOW:
            MOV     AL,[SI]             ; Character
;********************|
;   test for control |
;      characters    |
;********************|
            CMP     AL,00H              ; Terminator
            JE      SHOW_END
            CMP     AL,0FFH             ; End of line
            JE      LINE_END
; Display it by storing character in video buffer
            MOV     ES:[DI],AX          ; Store character and attribute
            INC     DL                  ; Next column
;********************|
;   bump pointer     |
;********************|
BUMP_PTRS:
            CALL    SET_DI              ; Next screen position
            INC     SI                  ; Bump message pointer
            JMP     GET_AND_SHOW
;********************|
;   end of line      |
;********************|
LINE_END:
            INC     DH                  ; Bump row pointer
            MOV     DL,CL               ; Reset column to start column
            JMP     BUMP_PTRS
;********************|
;   end of routine   |
;********************|
SHOW_END:
```

```
        POP     DX                  ; Restore registers
        POP     CX
        POP     AX
        CLC                         ; No error detection
        RET
SHOW_DIRECT     ENDP
;****************************************************************
;
CODE    ENDS
        END     ENTRY_POINT         ; Reference to label at which
                                    ; execution starts
```

VOCABULARY

alphanumeric modes	pointer register
color diplay	regen buffer
direct access	signed numbers
doubleword	system cursor
math coprocessor	unsigned numbers
memory mapped	video memory
monochrome display	virtual cursor

QUESTIONS

1. What is the address of the video buffer in a monchrome system?
2. What is the address of the video buffer in a color alphanumeric system?
3. What segment register is commonly used in accessing the video buffer directly?
4. What is the structure of the video buffer in the alphanumeric modes?
5. How can make the system cursor be made to disappear from the screen?
6. What is the difference between a signed and an unsigned operand?
7. What instruction can be used in adding two byte-size operands?
8. In which registers must the source operand be located for a MUL instruction?
9. Where is the doubleword product stored by the MUL instruction?
10. In which register is the byte quotient returned after a DIV instruction?

EXERCISES

1. Draw a flowchart for the SHOW_DIRECT procedure in the program LES-SON7.ASM

2. Design and code a version of the program LESSON7.ASM so that the characters in the range 80H to FFH are the only ones displayed. Reduce the frame and adjust the border digits as necessary. The displayed characters should appear centered on the screen.

3. Design and code a version of the program LESSON6.ASM using direct access to the video display. Hide the system cursor and replace it with a graphics cursor using the character DCH and a blinking attribute.

8

Interrupts, TSRs, and the System Timer

8.0 THE INTERRUPT SYSTEM ON IBM MICROCOMPUTERS

Most external devices in a computer system require attention from the central processor. For example, the keyboard, the video hardware, the printer, and the disk and diskette drives must occasionally use the services of the central processor. One of the mechanisms by which a hardware device can request the attention of the CPU is called an *interrupt*.

This is not the first time we meet the word "interrupt." In previous chapters we have used BIOS and MS-DOS programmer services located at various *software interrupts*. In this chapter we will discuss interrupts that are generated by a hardware device. This type of interrupt is often called *hardware interrupt*. When the interrupt signal is received the CPU immediately puts aside the task currently executing and responds to the interrupting device. The response is performed in a manner that will allow the resumption of the interrupted task.

In the IBM microcomputers we can identify the following types of interrupts.

1. *Software interrupts* can be of two types. The more common ones are those originated by an INT instruction. For example, we have used the BIOS video services via the instruction INT 10H. The second type of software interrupt is the one generated by the interrupt on overflow instruction (INTO). This software interrupt, used mostly in mathematical error handlers, takes place only if the overflow flag is set.

2. *Internal interrupts* are those that originate inside the CPU. For example, if a DIV instruction executes with a zero value for the divisor, the microprocessor will automatically generate a division-by-zero interrupt. The single-step interrupt, used by debugger programs in the controlled execution of another program, is also an internal interrupt.

3. *External interrupts* are initiated by a hardware device. These interrupts are signaled to the CPU on one of two special lines: the interrupt request (INTR) or the nonmaskable interrupt (NMI) line.

Table 8.1 lists the most used interrupts in the IBM microcomputers.

TABLE 8.1 MAJOR INTERRUPTS ON IBM MICROCOMPUTERS

ADRESSS	TYPE	DESCRIPTION	
0000H	0H	Divide by zero	
0004H	1H	Single step	
0008H	2H	Nonmaskable interrupt (NMI)	
000CH	3H	Breakpoint	
0010H	4H	Interrupt-on-overflow (INTO)	
0014H	5H	Print screen	
0020H	8H	System time	IRQ0
0024H	9H	Keyboard handler	IRQ1
0028H	0AH	Reserved	IRQ2
002CH	0BH	Communications COM2 .	IRQ3
0030H	0CH	Communications COM1 .	IRQ4
0034H	0DH	Disk	IRQ5
0038H	0EH	Diskette	IRQ6
003CH	0FH	Printe	IRQ7
0040H	10H	Video functions	
0044H	11H	Equipment check	
0048H	12H	Memory size	
004CH	13H	Diskette and disk	
0050H	14H	Communications	
0054H	15H	Cassette (AT extended services)	
0058H	16H	Keyboard	
005CH	17H	Printer	
0060H	18H	Resident BASIC language	
0064H	19H	Bootstrap	
0068H	1AH	Time-of-day	
006CH	1BH	Keyboard break	
0070H	1CH	User timer tick	
0074H	1DH	Video parameters	AREA
0078H	1EH	Diskette parameters	AREA
007CH	1FH	Graphic characters	AREA
0080H	20H	DOS program terminate	
0084H	21H	DOS general service call	
0088H	22H	DOS terminate address	
008CH	23H	DOS control break exit address	
0090H	24H	DOS fatal error exit	
0094H	25H	DOS absolute disk read	
0098H	26H	DOS absolute disk write	
009CH	27H	DOS terminate-and-stay-resident	
0100H	40H	Diskette BIOS revector	
0104H	41H	Hard disk parameters	
0118H	46H	Hard disk parameters	
0128H	4AH	User alarm	
0180H	60H to 67H	Reserved for USER SOFTWARE	
01C0H	70H	Real time clock	
01D4H	75H	Math coprocessor	
01D8H	76H	Hard disk controller	
0200H	80H to F0H	Reserved or used by BASIC	
03C4H	F1H to FFH	Reserved for USER SOFTWARE	

8.1 INTERRUPT SERVICE ROUTINES

Upon receiving an interrupt signal the processor first tests if the interrupt was triggered by a breakpoint interrupt or by an interrupt-on-overflow instruction, because these interrupts are handled separately. If it was not triggered by either a breakpoint or an overflow condition, then the CPU uses the data provided in the interrupt opcode (sometimes called the *interrupt signature*) to calculate the address of the corresponding interrupt handler. An interrupt handler is a routine, particular to each interrupt, that resides anywhere in the system's memory. The address of each interrupt handler is stored in a reserved area of memory called the *interrupt vector table*.

The Interrupt Vector Table

The interrupt vector table takes up 1024 bytes at the beginning of RAM, from physical address 00000H to 03FFH. The vector table holds the 4-byte addresses of all 256 possible service routines, one for each interrupt source. Each entry in the vector table is in the form of a logical address: the first 2 bytes encode the segment base and the last 2 bytes the offset. Because each address takes 4 bytes, the offset in the vector table for any particular interrupt can be calculated by multiplying the interrupt number by 4. For example, the address of the routine associated with the BIOS video services of interrupt 10H is found at offset 64 of the vector table, which can be calculated as follows:

$$10H = 16D$$
$$16 * 4 = 64$$

Considering that the vector table is used by the processor in obtaining the address of the interrupt service routines, it is easy to see how the mismanagement of this table can crash the entire system by sending execution to an undefined address.

The programmer must also keep in mind that not all interrupts have to be implemented in a particular system. In Table 8.1 we can see several areas that are not used for storing interrupt vectors, such as the pointers starting at offset 0074H, as well as other areas reserved for user interrupts and other purposes.

Regardless of the type, the INT instruction generates an interrupt to the vector contained in the operand. In other words, the instruction INT 00H executes a division-by-zero interrupt as if this condition had actually occurred in the microprocessor.

Interrupt Programming

Interrupt programming usually refers to one of the following operations:

1. To create a new service routine linked to an unassigned interrupt. For example, a programmer could develop a series of mathematical services and make these services available under interrupt 60H (see type in Table 8.1). Once the interrupt software is

installed, a program would be able to use these mathematical services in a similar manner as the BIOS video, keyboard, or printer services discussed in previous chapters.

2. To replace an existing interrupt service routine. For example, the developer of new video hardware could replace the BIOS video services offered by interrupt 10H with a set of routines adapted to the new system.

3. To intercept an existing interrupt service routine. For example, a program could disable the Caps Lock key by intercepting the system's keyboard service routine and discarding this keystroke.

MS-DOS Memory Management

We have seen that on the occurrence of an interrupt the CPU transfers execution to a routine, usually called the *interrupt handler*. The address of the interrupt handler is stored at the corresponding position in the vector table. Therefore, the interrupt handler must reside at a fixed memory address.

On the other hand, MS-DOS considers program memory as a reusable resource. When MS-DOS loads an executable program it will grant to it the necessary memory. When the executable program concludes, usually by means of MS-DOS service number 76 of interrupt 21H, this memory space is freed by MS-DOS so it can be reassigned. Consequently, we cannot use the standard MS-DOS loader to install an interrupt service routine if this routine is to reside at a fixed memory address so that it can be executed on the occurrence of the interrupt.

Programs that remain at a fixed memory area, protected from being reassigned by MS-DOS, are usually classified as *terminate-and-stay-resident* programs (TSR). MS-DOS includes services that allow the creation of TSR programs. Interrupt handlers that provide services to other software are coded as TSR. However, customized interrupt handlers that have no independent life outside of the program that they serve need not be in the form of a TSR.

Coding the TSR Routine

A TSR interrupt handler for the IBM microcomputers is usually formed by two separate routines. The *installation routine* takes over the interrupt vector and places the handler code in a protected memory space. The *service routine*, which gains control on the occurrence of the corresponding interrupt, performs the actual processing operations.

In developing and installing interrupt-driven code the programmer must be aware of the specific circumstances of this environment. One of them is that most hardware interrupts can occur at any time. For this reason, interrupts should be disabled while making changes in the vector table in order to avoid the risk of an interrupt taking place while there is no valid address for a service routine. The CLI (clear interrupt-enable flag) instruction, which disables all maskable interrupts, can be used for this purpose. The STI (set interrupt-enable flag) reenables the maskable interrupts. The following sequence of operations is usually recommended when installing an interrupt handler:

1. Disable interrupts.

2. Save the address of the old handler if an existing handler is being replaced.

3. Install the address of the new handler in the vector table.

4. Reenable interrupts.

5. Protect the memory space occupied by the new interrupt service routine and return control to MS-DOS.

The interrupt service routine usually executes the following operations:

1. Reenable interrupts. Note that the CPU automatically disables interrupts before transferring execution to the handler.

2. Save the machine registers used by the handler.

3. Perform handler operations.

4. Restore registers used by the handler.

5. Exit with an IRET (interrupt return) instruction if the handler substitutes the original service routine or return control to the original handler. This last operation is usually performed by means of a JMP to a variable holding the address of the original service routine.

TSR-Related Services in MS-DOS

MS DOS provides several services that are useful in developing TSR routines for interrupt handlers. The following are probably the most useful ones:

1. Service number 37 of interrupt 21H can be used to install the address of a new interrupt handler in the system's vector table.

2. Service number 53 of interrupt 21H can be used to retrieve, from the vector table, the address of an installed handler.

3. MS-DOS interrupt 27H, often called the TSR interrupt, allows terminating execution of a program while protecting all or part of its memory space so that it will not be reused by MS-DOS.

The COM-Type Program

We have mentioned that hardware interrupts can occur at any time. This means that the handler can make no assumptions regarding the contents of the microprocessor registers at the time that it receives control. By the same token, the handler cannot directly access external data, nor can it assume any depth in the stack.

There is a type of MS-DOS executable file named a *command program*, which, because of these restrictions, is often useful in coding stand-alone interrupt handlers. Command programs can be identified by the extension COM. The following are fundamental characteristics of a command program:

1. The code segment is relocatable (as in all MS-DOS programs); the first executable instruction must always be at offset 100H. The first 100H bytes are used by MS-DOS for storing program data.

2. The segment registers DS, ES, and SS are set by the loader to the value of the CS register. If enough memory is available, a 64-K stack is also created at load time.

3. The total length of the program cannot exceed 64K.

Command programs cannot contain segment relocations. This limitation forces the code to handle DS, ES, and SS directly. DOS interrupt 27H, often used to protect the memory space of an interrupt handler, requires that the CS register be set to the start of the PSP, which is the case with a command program.

Interrupt Intercepts

One type of interrupt service routine is designed to intercept the execution of an existing interrupt. In order to resume execution at the original service routine, the installation process of an *interrupt intercept* usually saves the original vector in its own memory space. This done, the intercept routine has two options: to restore processing at the original handler by means of a simple jump instruction, or to end the interrupt sequence by means of an IRET (interrupt return).

8.2 SYSTEM CLOCK AND TIMERS

All computer systems require a timed pulse in order to operate the digital circuitry. A timed signal is also required to synchronize the various electronic components so that they will maintain correct phase relations. Some microprocessor are equipped with a built-in clock that generates the system's pulse signal. However, in IBM microcomputers, the system clock is a separate chip. In addition to this clock generator, IBM microcomputers are equipped with a dedicated chip, driven by the system clock, that provides various timing services. The original integrated circuit (IC) timer used in the Personal Computer is the Intel 8253/54 Programmable Interval Timer. Although some models of the PS/2 line use a proprietary IBM timer chip, the IBM IC is software-compatible with the 8253/54.

The 8253/54 timer in the IBM microcomputers is designed to generate a wave frequency of 1.19318 megahertz (1,193,180 beats per second). In the PC line and some models of the PS/2 line, the timer has three internal and independent counters known as channels 0, 1, and 2. The Micro Channel models of the PS/2 line contain an additional channel designated with the number 3. In all IBM microcomputer systems timer channel 0 is connected to IRQ0 interrupt line (see Table 8.1). Each pulse of this channel generates an interrupt 08H, which is vectored to a handler located in the BIOS. Timer channel 0, which is also used in timing diskette motor operations, has a pulse rate of approximately 18.2 beats per second. Timer channel 1 is linked to the memory refresh mechanism in the IBM microcomputers that do not use Micro Channel architecture and is undocumented in Micro Channel systems. Timer channel 2 is routed to the internal speaker and used in generating sounds. Some of these timer channels are programmable and some are reserved for system use. The present discussion is limited to timer channel 0.

The Interrupt 08H Handler

In the IBM microcomputers timer channel 0 generates 18.2 pulses per second. This timer channel, which is connected to line number 0 (IRQ0) of the 8259 interrupt controller, generates an interrupt 08H at this rate. The interrupt handler, which is part of the BIOS program, maintains a count of these timer pulses and uses the count to keep track of time-of-day and the date. Some IBM microcomputers are equipped with a battery-powered clock that maintains the timer count when the system's main power switch is off.

The interrupt 08H handler, often called the system timer interrupt, is used also for diskette motor operations. In addition, on every clock tick, the interrupt 08H handler generates a software interrupt to the routine at vector 1CH. A user routine coded to intercept interrupt 1CH will receive control at every tick of the system timer. The program LESSON8.ASM at the end of this chapter uses this technique for timing a screen display operation.

8.3 ELEMENTS OF THE PROGRAM LESSON8.ASM

The program LESSON8.ASM is an interrupt intercept for the user timer tick at interrupt 1CH. The program uses direct access to the video display buffer to create an electronic billboard effect on the top screen line. Direct access display is advantageous in this type of application considering that an interrupt handler should execute as rapidly as possible in order to minimize the disturbance to the code currently running.

The program is divided into an installation routine (see text reference # 1) and an interrupt service routine (see text reference #2). The operation performed by the service routine consists of displaying a text message on the top screen line on every other tick of the system timer. The code intentionally slows the display function to every other timer beat in order to produce a smoother animated effect. The actual animation is performed by successively changing that start position in the display buffer one character to the right. This produces the effect of a message being scrolled left on the screen. The message is copied twice into the display buffer by the installation routine so that there will always be at least 80 characters to the right of the starting position.

All program data in LESSON8.ASM are stored in the code segment (see listing). This is convenient because when an interrupt service routine receives control the segment registers DS, SS, and ES still hold the values used by the interrupted code. An alternative solution is to reset the segment register as the handler gains control. LESSON8.ASM performs this operation with ES so that this register can be used to address video memory. Because the data are located in the code segment, all data access instructions in the installation and the service routine must use the CS segment override byte.

The Installation Routine

The installation for LESSON8.ASM routines performs the following operations:

1. Obtains and saves in the program's data space the address of the original service routine for interrupt 1CH. The address is obtained using service number 53 of interrupt 21H (see text reference # 3). The intercept operation is performed as an illustration of this programming method, because interrupt 1CH was designed as a user service and does not require returning control to the original handler.

2. Activates the new service routine for interrupt 1CH by installing its address in the vector table. The code performs this operation using service number 37 of interrupt 21H (see text reference # 4).

3. Saves the base address of the video buffer in a memory variable (see text reference # 5). This operation is intended as a time saver for the intercept routine, which will not have to recalculate the video buffer base address on each iteration.

4. Prepares the display buffer by initializing the character and attribute codes and moves two copies of the 80-byte message into the 160-byte buffer area (see text reference # 6). This is necessary in order to produce an animated screen message by simply changing the start position in a 160-character buffer.

5. Protects the installed handler in memory using MS-DOS interrupt 27H (see text reference # 7). The protected code does not include the installation routine, which is intentionally placed at the end of the program.

The Service Routine

The interrupt handler is installed by executing the program named LESSON8.COM. Once in place, the interrupt service routine receives control at each tick of the system timer, approximately 18.2 times per second.

When an interrupt handler receives control the processor's interrupt enable flag is clear, thus disabling other interrupts. The first operation usually performed by the handler is to reenable interrupts by setting the interrupt flag. This is performed by the LESSON8.ASM program by means of the STI instruction (see text reference # 8).

The interrupt handler must restore the machine context to the interrupted routine in the same state as it received it. For this reason the handler must use the stack to store the entry values in all the machine registers that it will use. This operation is shown in text reference #9.

In order to make a smoother animated effect the display routine takes place at one half the rate of the timer beat. LESSON8.ASM uses the variable TOGGLE_CTRL (see text reference # 10) to keep track of every other timer beat. The processing required to skip every other timer cycle is shown in text reference # 11.

The display operation (text reference # 12) is performed by accessing the video buffer directly. This has the advantage of reducing the interference of the interrupt routine by implementing video output in the fastest possible manner. The routine obtains the base address of the video buffer from the variable VIDEO_BASE, where it was saved by the installation routine.

Once the message is displayed, the program restores the entry values in the machine registers (text reference # 13) and returns control to the original handler by means of jump instruction (see text reference # 14). In this particular application the JMP instruction is not strictly necessary, because interrupt 1CH is specifically designed as a user intercept. This means that the processing could have also concluded satisfactorily by means of a simple IRET (interrupt return) instruction.

8.4 SOURCE CODE LISTING OF THE PROGRAM LESSON8.ASM

```
;****************************************************************
;****************************************************************
;                         LESSON8.ASM
;****************************************************************
;****************************************************************
; Program title: LESSON8
; Start date:
; Last modification:
;
; Program description:
; Simulation of an electronic billboard on the top screen line
; Program uses direct access to the video buffer
; Executable file must be a command-type program
;
; Note:
; The animation effect is created by copying an 80-character
; message (BILL_MSG) twice into a 160-character buffer named
; (MSG_BUFFER). A pointer (LAST_POS) signals the first character
; to be displayed during the present iteration. The pointer is
; bumped at every iteration and rewound when it reaches the first
; character of the second copy of the message.
;
; DOS commands for creating the run file LESSON8.COM
;       1. MASM LESSON8;
;       2. LINK LESSON8;
```

```
;           3. EXE2BIN LESSON8.EXE LESSON8.COM
;           4. ERASE LESSON8.EXE
;
; New operations:
;           1. Intercepting an interrupt
;           2. Storing data in the code segment
;           3. Coding an interrupt handler
;           4. Animation by consecutive imaging
;           5. Returning control to the original handler
;
;****************************************************************
;                         code segment
;****************************************************************
;
CODE    SEGMENT

        ORG     0100H           ; COM file forced origin

        ASSUME  CS:CODE,DS:CODE,ES:CODE,SS:CODE
;
ENTRY:
        JMP     INSTALL
;
;****************************************************************
;                       code segment data
;****************************************************************
OLD1C_ADD       DW      ?                       ; Offset of old vector
OLD1C_SEG       DW      ?                       ; Segment of old vector
;
VIDEO_BASE      DW      0B000H  ; Address of video buffer
;
; Video buffer for holding the message to be displayed
MSG_BUFFER      DB      320 DUP (00H)
                DW      0FFFFH
;
; Text to be moved into the message buffer
BILL_MSG        DB      ' ***** Hamburger $2.35 ** Cheeseburger'
                DB      ' $3.00  **  Soft drinks $0.45 ** THANK'
                DB      ' YOU ** ',00H
;
LAST_POS        DW      0       ; Last offset of the video buffer
                                ; for starting display
```

```
;                                              |********************|
;                                              | text reference # 10 |
;                                              |********************|
TOGGLE_CTRL     DB      0         ; On/off control to slow display
;*****************************************************************
;              interrupt 1CH intercept routine
;*****************************************************************
;                                              |********************|
;                                              | text reference # 2 |
;                                              |********************|
HEX1C_INT:
; Interrupts on
;                                              |********************|
;                                              | text reference # 8 |
;                                              |********************|
        STI                 ; Re-enable interrupts
;                                              |********************|
;                                              | text reference # 9 |
;                                              |********************|
;********************|
;    save context    |
;********************|
; Save all registers used by the interrupt intercept routine
; including the ES segment register
        PUSH    AX
        PUSH    CX
        PUSH    SI
        PUSH    DI
        PUSH    ES
;                                              |********************|
;                                              | text reference # 11 |
;                                              |********************|
;********************|
;  test toggle byte  |
;********************|
; The byte at TOGGLE_CTRL is changed to 0 or 1 in each iteration
; Display function is bypassed when value is 1, thereby slowing
; down the animation
        MOV     AL,CS:TOGGLE_CTRL        ; Get byte
        CMP     AL,1            ; Test for skip value
        JE      SKIP_ITER       ; Skip display of this iteration
; At this point TOGGLE_CTRL = 0. Change to 1 and execute display
```

```
; operation
        MOV     CS:TOGGLE_CTRL,1        ; Toggle to 1
        JMP     DISPLAY_IT              ; Go to display routine
;**********************|
;   skip display       |
;**********************|
SKIP_ITER:
        MOV     CS:TOGGLE_CTRL,0        ; Toggle to 0
        JMP     RESTORE_AND_EXIT
;**********************|
;   update starting    |
;       location       |
;**********************|
;                                      |**********************|
;                                      | text reference # 12  |
;                                      |**********************|
DISPLAY_IT:
; Set DS to video buffer address
        MOV     AX,CS:VIDEO_BASE ; Segment address of video buffer
        MOV     ES,AX
; Calculate address of the video buffer where display will start
; using the value stored at LAST_POS
        INC     CS:LAST_POS       ; Bump start position in buffer
        LEA     SI,CS:MSG_BUFFER; Pointer to buffer
        MOV     AX,CS:LAST_POS    ; Offset of this display position
        ADD     AX,AX             ; Double the offset
        CMP     AX,160            ; Test for last position in the
                                  ; buffer
        JNE     OK_SHOW           ; Go if not the last byte
        MOV     CS:LAST_POS,0     ; Reset counter
OK_SHOW:
        ADD     SI,AX             ; Add offset of this starting
                                  ; position to start of buffer
;**********************|
;   display buffer     |
;**********************|
        MOV     DI,0              ; First screen row and column
        MOV     CX,80             ; 80 words to move
DISPLAY_80:
        MOV     AX,WORD PTR CS:[SI]       ; Get source word
        MOV     WORD PTR ES:[DI],AX       ; Display it
        ADD     SI,2              ; Bump pointers twice
```

```
        ADD     DI,2
        LOOP    DISPLAY_80
;*********************|
;    exit routine     |
;*********************|
;                                          |*********************|
;                                          | text reference # 13 |
;                                          |*********************|
RESTORE_AND_EXIT:
        POP     ES              ; Restore ES segment
        POP     DI              ; and general registers
        POP     SI
        POP     CX
        POP     AX
;                                          |*********************|
;                                          | text reference # 14 |
;                                          |*********************|
; Exit from new service routine to old service routine
        JMP     DWORD PTR CS:OLD1C_ADD
;****************************************************************
;                    installation routine
;****************************************************************
; Installation consists of the following steps:
; 1. Obtain address of original service routine for INT 1CH
;      and save in the new handler's data space
; 2. Install the address of the new intercept routine in the
;      interrupt vector table
; 3. Save base address of the video buffer in a memory variable
;      for use by the service routine
; 4. Initialize the buffer containing the message to be displayed
;      by the service routine
; 5. Protect the installed handler and return control to MS-DOS
;
INSTALL:
        CLI
;                                          |*********************|
;                                          | text reference # 1  |
;                                          |*********************|
;*********************|
;  get address of old |
;       handler       |
;*********************|
```

```
; Uses MS-DOS service 53 of interrupt 21H to obtain the original
; address for INT 1CH
;                                        |*********************|
;                                        |  text reference # 3 |
;                                        |*********************|
        MOV     AH,53           ; Service request code
        MOV     AL,1CH          ; Code of vector desired
        INT     21H
; ES -> Segment address of installed interrupt handler
; BX -> Offset address of installed interrupt handler
        MOV     CS:OLD1C_ADD,BX ; Store offset in variable
        MOV     CS:OLD1C_SEG,ES ; Store segment base
;                                        |*********************|
;                                        |  text reference # 4 |
;                                        |*********************|
;*********************|
; install new handler |
;*********************|
; Take over timer tick at INT 1CH Using DOS service 37 of
; interrupt 21H
        MOV     AH,37           ; Service request number
        MOV     AL,1CH          ; Interrupt to be intercepted
        LEA     DX,CS:HEX1C_INT ; Pointer to handler
        INT     21H             ; MS-DOS interrupt
;                                        |*********************|
;                                        |  text reference # 5 |
;                                        |*********************|
;*********************|
;  store base address |
;    of video buffer  |
;*********************|
; Default video buffer base is B000H. Test system and change
; base if video hardware is a color card
        MOV     AX,0040H        ; Segment base of BIOS data area
        MOV     ES,AX           ; To ES
        MOV     AX,ES:[0010H]   ; Get equipment word at offset
                                ; 0010H
        AND     AX,00110000B    ; Mask off all bits except 4 and
                                ; 5
        CMP     AL,00110000B    ; Test for xx11 xxxx pattern
        JE      MONO_SYS        ; Monochrome card installed
; At this point the video hardware is a color system. Base
```

```
; address of video buffer, stored in the variable VIDEO_BASE,
; must be changed to B800H
        MOV     AX,0B800H          ; Screen address of color systems
        MOV     CS:VIDEO_BASE,AX
;                                         |********************|
;                                         | text reference # 6 |
;                                         |********************|
;********************|
;  initialize message |
;        buffer        |
;********************|
; Format the buffer MSG_BUFFER with blanks and normal attributes
MONO_SYS:
        MOV     AL,20H             ; Character
        MOV     AH,07H             ; Normal display attribute
        MOV     DI,OFFSET CS:MSG_BUFFER
        MOV     CX,160             ; Total words in buffer
TO_BUFFER:
        MOV     CS:[DI],AX         ; Word to buffer
        ADD     DI,2               ; Bump pointer to next address
        LOOP    TO_BUFFER          ; Repeat 160 times
; Move 3 copies of the message to be displayed into the display
; buffer
        LEA     DI,CS:MSG_BUFFER           ; Pointer to buffer
PUT_MSG:
        MOV     SI,OFFSET CS:BILL_MSG    ; Text message
        LEA     SI,CS:BILL_MSG           ; Message to be displayed
        MOV     CX,80                    ; 80 bytes long
PUT_80:
        MOV     AL,CS:[SI]         ; Get message character
        MOV     CS:[DI],AL         ; Move character into buffer
        ADD     DI,2               ; Bump video buffer pointer
        INC     SI                 ; and message pointer
        CMP     BYTE PTR CS:[DI],0FFH
                                   ; FFH is end of buffer mark
        JE      MSG_END
        LOOP    PUT_80             ; Place 80 characters
        JMP     PUT_MSG
;                                         |********************|
;                                         | text reference # 7 |
;                                         |********************|
;
```

```
;*********************|
;   protect routine   |
;        and exit     |
;*********************|
; Exit to DOS protecting the service routine above the label
; INSTALL using MS-DOS interrupt 27H
MSG_END:
        STI
        MOV     DX,OFFSET CS:INSTALL     ; Start protection
        INC     DX              ; Add 1 byte
        INT     27H             ; MS-DOS service
CODE    ENDS
        END     ENTRY
```

VOCABULARY

command program   interrupt intercept
hardware interrupt   interrupt signature
interrupt   interrupt vector table
interrupt handler   software interrupt
TSR

QUESTIONS

1. List the names of the three types of interrupts.
2. What is the use of the interrupt signature?
3. What can occur if the interrupt vector table is mismanaged?
4. Write the formula for calculating the address of an interrupt service routine in the vector table.
5. What is the purpose of an interrupt intercept routine?
6. What words were used in the acronym "TSR"?
7. How can the interrupt handler disable interrupts?
8. List three characteristics of a command program.
9. To which interrupt line is the timer connected in the IBM microcomputers?
10. What interrupt handler is associated with the system timer?

EXERCISES

1. Draw a flowchart of the interrupt 1CH intercept routine in the program LESSON8.ASM.

2. Design and code a version of the program LESSON8.ASM in which the message is displayed at the last 20 display positions of the bottom screen line. Replace the message text with one that occupies the entire 240 character bytes in the display buffer.

3. Design and code an intercept routine for interrupt 08H. Use the timer tick to maintain a seconds counter. Recycle the counter when the value reaches 99 seconds. Display the two-digit ASCII value of the seconds counter at the top right corner of the screen. Update the displayed value every second.

9

Serial Communications

9.0 THE SERIAL PORT

The main communications link of an IBM microcomputer with the outside world is the serial port. The machine transmits and receives data from other computers and from many devices by way of a multiple-wire connector that links the serial ports. The term *RS-232-C port* is often used as a synonym for serial port. RS-232-C is a communications standard developed by the Electronics Industries Association (EIA) for serial communications (Recommended Standard 232, Revision C).

In serial communications data is encoded in a stream of consecutive electrical pulses that are sent through a single communications line. This differs from the method used in parallel communications (see Section 6.1), in which data is sent simultaneously over several lines. Note that although serial communications use a single transmission line for sending operations, there is a separate line for receiving data as well as other ground and control lines. The control lines are used in a synchronization function called *handshaking*.

The RS-232-C Standard

For serial communications to take place the sending and the receiving devices must agree on certain physical parameters, such as the speed at which the transmission is to take place, the number and function of the control bits, and the number of bits used to encode the data. These parameters are usually called the *communications protocol*. The EIA has sponsored the development of several standards for serial communications. One of them, named RS-232-C, is an easy-to-implement voltage convention that is used in the serial port of the IBM microcomputers.

The following terms are used in serial communications according to the RS-232-C standard:

1. The *baud rate* is a measurement of the speed of transmission. The term is commonly interpreted to mean bits per second, although technically the baud rate refers to the switching speed of the transmission line. Serial communications require that the transmitter and the receiver clocks be synchronized to the same baud period. In IBM microcomputers the most frequently used baud rates are 110, 300, 600, 1200, 2400, 4800, 9600, and 19200.

2. The *start bit* is a transmission pulse that serves to mark the start of a data transmission.

3. The *character bits* are a group of 5, 6, 7, or 8 bits used to encode the data character.

4. The *parity bit* is an optional transmission pulse used in detecting errors. The RS-232-C standard allows *even parity*, *odd parity*, and *no parity*. Parity check is active only if the setting is odd or even.

IBM Microcomputer Serial Hardware

The IBM microcomputers' serial port can be part of the system board or contained in an optional adapter card. In the Personal Computer the serial port is an adapter card called the *Asynchronous Communications Adapter*. In the PC AT the serial card, which also contains a printer port, is called the *Serial/Parallel Adapter*. In the models of the PS/2 line and many IBM-compatible microcomputers the serial port is furnished as a standard component.

A machine can be equipped with more than one serial port. The BIOS designation for the serial ports is 0-based. The first serial port is labeled port number 0, the second port as number 1, and so on up to four possible ports. In MS-DOS the serial ports are designated using the abbreviation COM and a 1-based numbering system. In this manner, to MS-DOS the first serial port is labeled COM1, the second one COM2, and so forth. These different designations of the serial ports can be the source of program errors.

9.1 SERIAL COMMUNICATIONS METHODS

Serial communications are said to take place *asynchronously*. This means that the unit of transmission is a complete character and that it contains its own synchronization data. The fact that there is no general synchronization in the data transmission creates some programming problems. For example, if the received character is not removed fast enough from a holding register, the next character transmitted will overwrite and destroy it. In the following paragraphs we briefly discuss several methods that are regularly used to implement asynchronous communications.

Polling

The word "polling" is used in communications to describe a programming technique by which the receiving device checks the status of the transmission line at certain time frequency. The polling frequency must be sufficiently short to ensure that the transmitting device will not send a new character before the previous one has been removed. This means that the faster the speed of communications the more frequently the line must be polled.

Polling techniques are quite satisfactory at the slower transmission rates or regarding manual or mechanical devices. In the program LESSON9.ASM at the end of this chapter we have used polling to implement simultaneous reception and transmission of characters typed on the keyboard and received through the serial line. In this application even the fastest imaginable typist could never exceed the polling rate of the software.

But polling techniques often fail in applications where the transmission speed is not limited by a slow device. For example, a polled routine used in receiving memory data or disk files could lose characters during the period in which the receiver is forced to ignore the transmission line in order to store or display the characters acquired. In fact, practically all data losses in polled communications can be traced to the receiving terminal. Another limitation of polling is that the receiver must be an *intelligent* device. Polling is not possible when programming printers or *dumb* terminals.

Handshaking

Data losses in polled systems can be eliminated if the sender can be instructed to suspend the transmission while the receiver is performing other functions. The command exchange between sender and receiver in a communications system is called *handshaking*. A typical example of handshaking is a serial printer that forces the computer to stop sending until the previous character has been transferred to paper.

When the handshake code or command is transmitted by physical means, for instance, by changing a signal on a connecting wire, it is classified as a *hardware handshaking*. A simple hardware handshake protocol uses two signals, named *data set ready* (DSR) and *data terminal ready* (DTR). In this case the device (for example, a serial printer) will raise the DTR line to inform the computer that it is ready to receive. If the printer wants to suspend transmission, it will lower DTR to a negative voltage.

Software Handshake

Many serial devices are connected using simple wiring schemes in which the control lines have been eliminated. One such scheme, known as a *null modem* wiring, uses one line to transmit data, another line to receive data, and a common ground. Because there are no control lines in a null modem design, it is impossible to use any form of hardware handshake. In this case, synchronization between sender and receiver can be implemented by means of special codes transmitted through the data lines. Code conventions for synchronizing serial communications are often called a *software handshake*.

One of the more popular software handshake conventions is the XON/XOFF protocol. In this communications protocol the character 13H (XOFF) is used to signal the transmitting device to stop sending characters, and the character 17H (XON) is used to signal that transmission can resume. Because the control codes are inserted in the data stream, these characters cannot be used for other purposes. In the ASCII encoding (see Appendix C) the alphanumeric characters are represented by codes starting at 20H. Therefore, a program can use control codes smaller than 20H to transmit ASCII files.

On the other hand, non-ASCII data, such as executable files or graphic images, often contain all possible bit combinations, including the control codes mentioned above. The receiver cannot differentiate these codes from other data items. For this reason, in the transmission of binary data, it is necessary to use other serial transmission schemes that allow handshaking without embedding control characters in the data stream. One scheme is to pack the binary data into discrete units — say, of 128 bytes. The control codes can then be used to synchronize the transmission and reception of each 128-byte data package, but no control codes are embedded in the data package itself. The XMODEM convention provides a data package file transfer protocol, with handshaking.

Communications Interrupts

Still another way to synchronize transmitter and receiver during data communications is by using the interrupt mechanism of the IBM microcomputers (see Chapter 8). This method, which is the most elaborate to implement, is also the one with best performance and data reliability. The basic approach is to program the communications hardware so that an interrupt is generated whenever a data item is received. The action can be described as giving the microprocessor a *tap on the shoulder* to let it know that a data byte was acquired. The CPU then interrupts whatever it is doing long enough to remove this byte from the receiver data register and place it in a safe storage location, where it will not be destroyed by the next reception. Due to their complexity serial communications using interrupts are not considered in this book.

9.2 SERIAL CONNECTION OF IBM MICROCOMPUTERS

Some form of wiring is always necessary to establish serial communications between two computers or between a computer and a serial device. The RS-232-C standard specifies a 25-pin hardware connector called a D-shell, or DB-25. But not all IBM serial ports use the DB-25 connector. For example, the PCjr serial port uses a 16-pin BERG connector and the PC AT Serial/Parallel Adapter uses a 9-pin D-shell. The same applies to IBM-compatible machines.

The simplest wiring scheme that allows connecting two computers through the serial port is called the null modem (see Section 9.1). In order to use the communication program LESSON9.ASM listed in this chapter (or any other serial communications software for that matter) it is first necessary to connect two IBM microcomputers by means of a null modem cable. Null modem cables for any two types of serial connectors can often be purchased at electronic parts stores. In any case, we provide the necessary information in this chapter so that, if the particular null modem cable is not available, the student may construct it or order one custom made.

Figure 9.1 is a diagram of the IBM serial connectors as seen from the back of the system unit.

DB-25 (Personal Computer, PC XT and PS/2 systems)

DB-9 (PC AT Serial/Parallel Adapter)

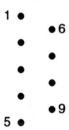

16-pin BERG (PCjr)

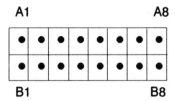

Figure 9.1 Digrams for IBM Microcomputer Serial Connectors

IBM and IBM-compatible microcomputers use one of the three serial connectors in Figure 9.1. Table 9.1 lists the lines on these serial connectors that are used in the simplest null modem wiring.

TABLE 9.1. NULL MODEM LINES ON IBM MICROCOMPUTERS SERIAL CONNECTORS

CONNECTOR			FUNCTION	DIRECTION
DB-25	DB-9	BERG		
2	3	A4	Transmit data	Output
3	2	A8	Receive data	Input
5	8	A7	Clear to send	Input
7	5	B1	Chassis ground	
8	1	A5	Carrier detect	
20	4	A2	Data terminal ready	Output

Note that not all serial lines have the same number designations in the various connectors. For example, the clear to send line corresponds with pin number 5 in a DB-25 connector, with pin number 8 on the DB-9 connector of the PC AT, and with pin number A7 on the BERG serial connectors of the IBM PCjr. The actual wiring diagram for the null modem cable is shown in Figure 9.2.

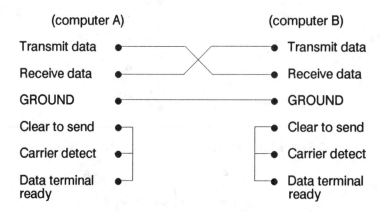

Figure 9.2 Wiring for a Null Modem Cable

In the wiring shown in Figure 9.2 only three lines are used in connecting the two computers. The null modem scheme requires the cross-connection of the transmit data and receive data lines as well as a common ground line. The clear to send, carrier detect, and data terminal ready pins are wired to one another inside the connector. The short cables used in these interconnections are called *jumpers*. The interconnected lines are sometimes said to be *dummied out*.

An actual wiring diagram for any adapter combination can be designed using the data in Figure 9.2 and Table 9.1. For example, to connect and IBM Personal Computer (DB-25 serial connector) to and IBM PC AT (DB-9 serial connector), the null modem cable will be as shown in Figure 9.3.

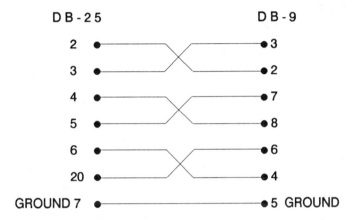

Figure 9.3 Null Modem Cable from PC (DB-25) to AT (DB-9)

9.3 PROGRAMMING SERIAL COMMUNICATIONS

Although some MS-DOS functions allow limited serial operations, most serial communications programs for the IBM microcomputers use BIOS serial services or access the communications hardware directly.

BIOS Serial Services

The BIOS program provides four services for programming serial communications, which are accessible under interrupt 14H. In general, these services are adequate for applications that execute at transmission rates not to exceed 1200 baud. Programs that perform display and storage operations while running at high transmission rates can lose data if the communications programming is performed by means of the BIOS serial services. The data losses can usually be traced to conditions in which a character arrives through the line before the previous one is removed from the holding register. The possibility for this type of error is related to the asynchronous nature of serial communications. The following are the BIOS serial communications services:

1. BIOS Service Number 0 of interrupt 14H. This service initializes the communications protocol according to the RS-232-C standard. The set-up values include baud rate, parity, stop bits, and word length (see Appendix A). Note that in all BIOS services of interrupt 14H the DX register is loaded with the zero-based number of the serial port. This means that a program addressing the default serial port (COM1) will load DX with zero.

2. BIOS Service Number 1 of interrupt 14H. This service is used to transmit a character through the serial communications line. The following fragment shows the processing required for transmitting the letter A.

```
MOV     AL,'A'          ; Character to be sent
MOV     AH,1            ; Service request number
MOV     DX,0            ; Communications port COM1
INT     14H             ; BIOS serial interrupt
```

When service number 1 returns to the caller the AH register contains the port status (see Appendix A). If bit 7 of AH is set, then the data byte was not transmitted.

3. BIOS Service Number 2 of interrupt 14H. This service is used to receive one character through the serial port. As in all serial services the port number must be passed in the DX register. The character received is returned in AL.

4. BIOS Service Number 3 of interrupt 14H. This service is used to obtain the status of the serial port. The AH register reports the status of the communications line and the AL register the modem status.

In addition to their relative slowness, the use of BIOS serial services can present the programmer with other problems. For example, service number 1 of interrupt 14H, to send a character, will wait for the data set ready and the clear to send signals before transmitting. If two computers are connected via a null modem wire (see the wiring diagram in Figure 9.2), the clear to send line is dummied out and the data set ready line is not used. This means that BIOS service number 1 will fail because these signals will never be correct. Due to this problem, in the program LESSON9.ASM we use direct access to the serial port for sending characters through the line.

Direct Access to the Serial Port

The fundamental electronic component of the serial port in the IBM microcomputers is the 8250 Universal Asynchronous Receiver and Transmitter (UART) or a functionally equivalent chip. Figure 9.4 is a diagram of the programmable components and the data flow in this controller.

The operation of the serial communications controller can be described as follows:

1. The transmitter portion of the controller converts an 8-bit data value, placed by the processor in the adapter's output port, into a serial bit stream formatted according to the RS-232-C protocol. During transmission the controller inserts the necessary start, stop, and parity bits.

    2. The controller can simultaneously decode an incoming bit stream and place the data byte in the adapter's input port (the receiver data register in Figure 9.4). The CPU can obtain the received data by reading this register. During reception the chip uses the start, stop, and parity bits to synchronize the transmission, to identify the data bits, and to check for errors.

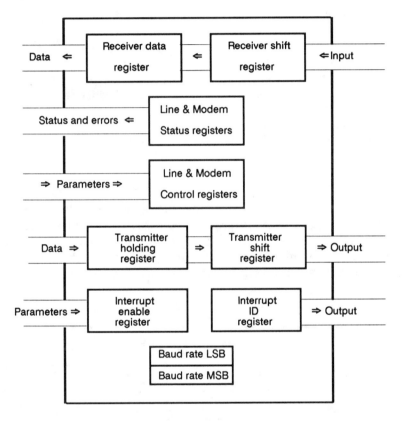

Figure 9.4 Registers and Operations of the Serial Serial Communications Controllers in the IBM Microcomputers

The Serial Port Address

Some IBM microcomputers can contain more than one serial port. In addition, other models (such as the PCjr) map the serial ports to different addresses. For these reasons, a serial communication program should not assume that the port is located at a certain physical address. In addressing any of the serial ports, the software can obtain the port's base address from the BIOS data area. The base address of the first serial port (COM1) is stored during the BIOS initialization at 400H in the BIOS data area. If additional ports are present in the system, their base addresses are stored at memory location 402H, 404H, and 406H. If one of these fields contains zero, then the corresponding port is not present in the system. The following code fragment shows the operations required for obtaining the base address of the first serial port (COM1):

```
; Obtain base address of COM1 from BIOS logical address
; 0000:0400H
        PUSH    ES              ; Save program's ES segment
        XOR     AX,AX           ; AX = 0
        MOV     ES,AX           ; Set ES to segment base
        MOV     DX,ES:0400H     ; Base address of COM1
        POP     ES              ; Restore segment register
; At this point DX has the port address
; A value of 0 will indicate no available serial hardware
```

The Controller's Registers

The 8250 UART and compatible communications controllers used in the IBM micro-computers appear to the programmer as consisting of 10 programmable registers. The central processor gains access to the controller through ports located at the base address or at a certain offset from the base address. Table 9.2 shows the port mapping and functions of the various registers in the serial communications controller.

TABLE 9.2 PROGRAMMABLE REGISTES IN THE IBM SERIAL CONTROLLERS

REGISTER	CODE NAME	COM1 ADDRESS BASE	OFFSET	FUNCTION
Transmitter holding register	THR	3F8H	0	OUTPUT
Receiver data register	RDR	3F8H	0	INPUT
Baud rate divisor (LSB)	BRDL	3F8H	0	OUTPUT
Baud rate divisor (MSB)	BRDH	3F9H	1	OUTPUT
Interrupt enable register	IER	3F9H	1	OUTPUT
Interrupt ID register	IID	3FAH	2	INPUT
Line control register	LCR	3FBH	3	OUTPUT
Modem control register	MDC	3FCH	4	OUTPUT
Line status register	LST	3FDH	5	INPUT
Modem status register	MSR	3FEH	6	INPUT

Note that the receiver shift register and the transmitter shift register in Figure 9.4 are not listed in Table 9.2. The reason is that these registers are not accessible to the programmer.

The *transmitter holding register* (THR) contains the character ready to be sent. To transmit a character through the serial port the program simply places the desired code in the port address (see Table 9.2) of the transmitter holding register.

The *receiver data register* (RDR) contains the character received through the communications line. To input a data byte received through the serial port the code reads the port address of the receiver data register.

The *baud rate divisor registers* are used to program the baud rate generator in the serial communications controller. One baud rate divisor register (BRDL) stores the least significant byte (see Table 9.2) and the following register (BRDH) stores the most significant byte of the baud rate. Because the baud rate can be effectively set using BIOS service number 0 of interrupt 14H, the details of programming the baud rate divisor registers directly are not considered in this book.

The *interrupt enable register* (IER) is used in relation to four types of hardware interrupts allowed by the serial communications controllers. The IER permits activating one or more of these interrupt sources. The *interrupt identification register* (IID) stores a priority code that makes possible the identification of one or more pending interrupts. Serial communications using interrupts are not considered in this book.

The *line control register* (LCR) performs two separate functions. The high bit of this register, often called the *divisor latch access bit* (DLAB), is used to select among various registers when they are mapped to the same address. If the DLAB bit is set, then read or write operations to the registers mapped to the base address will access the baud rate divisor LSB register. Also, read and write operations to the base address plus one will access the baud rate divisor LSB register. On the other hand, if the DLAB bit is clear, write operations to the base address will access the transmitter holding register and read operations will access the receiver data register. In this case read and write operations to the base address plus one will access the interrupt enable register. The second function of the line control register is in setting the communications protocol. In the present book we will set the protocol parameters using BIOS service number 0 of interrupt 14H.

The *modem control register* (MCR) is used in setting the handshake protocol when communicating with a modem or with a device that emulates a modem. Bits 0 and 1 of the modem control register control the data terminal ready (DTR) and the request to send (RTS) signals. When these bits are set, DTR and RTS become active. Bit 3 of this register controls the output 2 signal. This signal allows the interrupts generated by the communications controller to reach the interrupt controller.

The *line status register* (LSR) provides the CPU with information about the state of the data transfer operations. The function of each bit in the line status register is shown in Figure 9.5.

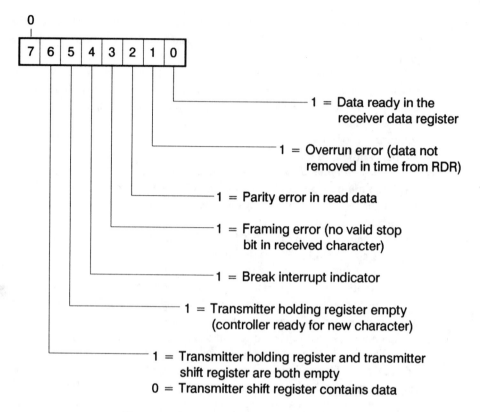

Figure 9.5 Bit Map of the Line Status Register

The *modem status register* (MSR) provides the CPU with information about the state of the control lines from the modem or modemlike device. Modem programming is not considered in this book.

Sending and Receiving Serial Data

Code that performs sending or receiving operations can use the line status register at the port's base address plus 5 (see Figure 9.5) to determine if the controller is ready for input or output. In case of sending data the program reads the byte at the line status register and tests if the transmitter holding register bit (bit number 5) is set to determine if a new character can be placed in the holding register. In case of receiving data the program tests bit 1 of the line status register to determine if there are data ready to be read in the receiver data register. The coding for a sending operation is shown in the program LESSON9.ASM (see text reference # 1). The following code fragment shows the operations required for receiving a data character through the serial line:

```
; Code for obtaining a data character received through the
; serial line. The code assumes that the base address of the
; serial port is stored in a word variable named PORT_BASE
DATA_CHECK:
        MOV     DX,PORT_BASE    ; Base address of serial port
        ADD     DX,5            ; Add offset of LSR
        IN      AL,DX           ; Read byte in LSR
        JMP     SHORT $+2       ; I/O delay instruction
; Check for data ready on line
        TEST    AL,00000001B    ; Test bit 0 (data ready bit)
        JNZ     DATA_READY      ; Go if bit set
; Check for error bits 1, 2, 3, and 4 (see Table 9.4)
        TEST    AL,00011110B    ; An error bit set ?
        JNZ     DATA_ERROR      ; Go to error handler
        JMP     DATA_CHECK      ; Continue testing line
; At this point there is an error in data reception. The error
; is reported by loading a question mark in the AL register
DATA_ERROR:
        MOV     AL,'?'          ; Error symbol
        JMP     READ_END        ; End of routine
; At this point there is data ready in the Receiver Data register
DATA_READY:
        MOV     DX,PORT_BASE    ; Base address is RDR register
                                ; during read operations
        IN      AL,DX           ; Get data byte
        JMP     SHORT $+2       ; I/O delay
; End of read routine. Data or error code in AL
READ_END:
        .
        .
        .
```

9.4 ELEMENTS OF THE PROGRAM LESSON9.ASM

LESSON9.ASM is a terminal communications program that allows the use of two IBM microcomputers, connected through the serial port via a null modem cable, to communicate with each other. The characters typed on the keyboard are automatically transmitted though the serial port. The characters received through the port are automatically displayed on the screen. This means that the send and receive functions are live at all times.

Obtaining the Serial Port Address

The program LESSON9.ASM obtains the base address of the serial port from the BIOS data storage word at logical address 0000:0400H (see text reference # 2). This base address is stored in a data segment variable so it can later be recovered by the program code.

Setting the Communications Protocol

The serial communications protocol parameters, baud rate, parity, number of stop bits, and word length are set using BIOS service number 0 of interrupt 14H (see text reference # 3). This service is described in Appendix A.

Flushing the Keyboard Buffer

Programs that use keyboard services often assume that the keyboard buffer in the BIOS data area is empty as the program executes, that is, that there are no pending keystrokes stored in this area. By flushing the buffer the code can also make certain that there are no pending characters. The operation can be performed using BIOS service number 1 to determine if there are characters pending to be read and BIOS service number 0 to discard any pending character. The programming is shown in text reference # 4 of LESSON9.ASM.

Polling Operations

In order to maintain live keyboard and serial reception the program LESSON9.ASM polls both devices in an endless loop (see text reference # 5). The only exit out of the loop takes place when the user presses the < Esc > key (see text reference # 6). The code first tests for a character pending in the keyboard buffer. This is done using service number 1 of interrupt 16H. If a character has been typed, and it is not the < Esc > key, it is displayed on the screen and sent through the serial port (see text reference # 7). The send operation uses direct access to the serial port so that the program can be used with a null modem cable (see Section 9.3). If the polling routine detects that a character is ready in the receiver data register, then it is fetched and displayed.

9.5 SOURCE CODE LISTING OF THE PROGRAM LESSON9.ASM

```
;******************************************************************
;******************************************************************
;                         LESSON9.ASM
;******************************************************************
```

```
;****************************************************************
; Program title: LESSON9
; Start date:
; Last modification:
;
; Program description:
; Serial communications using BIOS services and direct output to
; the RS-232-C port. Program transmits all characters typed on
; the keyboard and displays all characters received through the
; serial line
;
; New operations:
; 1. Obtaining the serial port address
; 2. Setting the communications protocol
; 3. Flushing the keyboard buffer
; 4. Polling the keyboard and the communications line
; 5. Sending characters through the serial port
; 6. Receiving characters through the serial port
;
;****************************************************************
;                         stack segment
;****************************************************************
STACK    SEGMENT stack
;
                DB      1024 DUP ('?')  ; Default stack is 1K
STACK    ENDS
;
;****************************************************************
;                         data segment
;****************************************************************
DATA     SEGMENT
;
MENU_MS DB       ' Serial Communications Program ',0AH,0DH
        DB       ' *** Press <Esc> to end ***',0AH,0DH,'$'
;
ERR1_MS DB       0DH,0AH,'  *** Cannot transmit *** '
        DB       0DH,0AH.'$'
;
; PROGRAM PARAMETER STORAGE:
PORT_BASE       DW      03F8H   ; Address of RS 232-C card
                                ; for all hardware types except
                                ; PCjr (PCjr = 02F8H)
```

```
;
DATA     ENDS
;****************************************************************
;                            code segment
;****************************************************************
;
CODE     SEGMENT
         ASSUME  CS:CODE
;*********************|
;    initialization   |
;*********************|
ENTRY_POINT:
; Initialize the DATA segment so that the program can access the
; stored data items using the DS segment register
         MOV     AX,DATA             ; Address of DATA to AX
         MOV     DS,AX               ; and to DS
         ASSUME  DS:DATA             ; Assume directive so that
                                     ; the assembler defaults to DS
; Display MENU at cursor
         MOV     DX,OFFSET MENU_MS        ; Message
         CALL    DOS_DISPLAY         ; Local procedure
;                                          |********************|
;                                          | text reference # 2 |
;                                          |********************|
;*********************|
;   address of RS-232-C |
;         port          |
;*********************|
; Get base address of serial port COM1 from BIOS data word at
; 00400H
         MOV     DX,0                ; BIOS data area segment
         MOV     ES,DX               ; Data segment to BIOS area
         MOV     CX,ES:[0400H]       ; Address of serial port COM1
         MOV     PORT_BASE,CX        ; Store in variable
;                                          |********************|
;                                          | text reference # 3 |
;                                          |********************|
;*********************|
;  set serial protocol |
;*********************|
; Set serial communications protocol as follows:
; Bit mask: 101xxxxx ...... Baud = 2400
```

```
;             xxx11xxx ...... Parity = even
;             xxxxx0xx ...... Stop bits = 1
;             xxxxxx11 ...... Word length = 8
; Result =   10111011
;
        MOV     AL,10111011B    ; Control code
        MOV     AH,0            ; Service request number
        MOV     DX,0            ; COM1 serial port assumed
        INT     14H             ; BIOS serial interrupt
;                               |*******************|
;                               | text reference # 4 |
;                               |*******************|
;********************|
;   flush keyboard   |
;********************|
; Make sure that not stray characters are left in the keyboard
; buffer
FLUSH_1:
        MOV     AH,1            ; Service request number
        INT     16H             ; BIOS keyboard interrupt
        JZ      MONITOR         ; Go if nothing in buffer
; At this point there are old characters in the buffer. Flush
; one character and re test
        MOV     AH,0            ; Service request number
        INT     16H             ; BIOS keyboard interrupt
        JMP     FLUSH_1         ; Test again for clean buffer
;                               |*******************|
;                               | text reference # 5 |
;                               |*******************|
;**************************************|
;   poll for sent or received characters |
;**************************************|
MONITOR:
        MOV     AH,1            ; Code for read keyboard status
        INT     16H             ; BIOS service
        JNZ     CHAR_TYPED      ; Character in keyboard buffer
; At this point no character has been typed on the keyboard
;********************|
; character received ? |
;********************|
; Use BIOS serial port status service to determine if there is
; data ready
```

```
                MOV     AH,3             ; Service request number
                MOV     DX,0             ; COM1
                INT     14H              ; BIOS serial interrupt
; Test data ready bit (bit 0)
                TEST    AH,00000001B     ; Test bit 0
                JNZ     GET_ONE          ; Go if bit set
                JMP     MONITOR          ; Nothing received
GET_ONE:
                MOV     AH,2             ; Service request number
                MOV     DX,0             ; COM1
                INT     14H              ; BIOS serial interrupt
; Received character is in AL
                CALL    SERIAL_TTY       ; Local procedure
                JMP     MONITOR
;                                        |********************|
;                                        | text reference # 7 |
;                                        |********************|
;********************|
;    get character in  |
;    keyboard buffer   |
;********************|
CHAR_TYPED:
                MOV     AH,0             ; Code for read keyboard char.
                INT     16H              ; BIOS service
;                                        |********************|
;                                        | text reference # 6 |
;                                        |********************|
;********************|
;   test for <Esc> key |
;********************|
                CMP     AX,011BH         ; Code for <Esc> key
                JE      DOS_EXIT
;                                        |********************|
;                                        | text reference # 1 |
;                                        |********************|
;********************|
;   display and send   |
;       character      |
;********************|
; At this point a character has been typed on the keyboard
; Send through RS-232-C line
; Wait loop for Transmitter Holding register empty
```

```
              MOV     CX,1000         ; Count for 1000 wait cycles
              PUSH    AX              ; Save character to transmit
              MOV     DX,PORT_BASE
              ADD     DX,5            ; Line status register
WAIT_FOR_THRE:
              IN      AL,DX           ; Get byte at port
              JMP     SHORT $+2       ; I/O delay
              TEST    AL,00100000B    ; Is the Transmitter Holding
                                      ; register empty ?
              JNZ     OK_2_SEND       ; Go if empty
              LOOP    WAIT_FOR_THRE   ; Wait if not empty
; Transmission not possible. Display error message
              POP     AX              ; Restore stack
              LEA     DX,ERR1_MS      ; Pointer to error message
              CALL    DOS_DISPLAY     ; Error to screen
              JMP     MONITOR
OK_2_SEND:
              POP     AX              ; Retrieve byte
; Place in transmitter holding register to send
              MOV     DX,PORT_BASE    ; THR
              OUT     DX,AL           ; Send
              JMP     SHORT $+2       ; I/O delay
; Display character
              CALL    SERIAL_TTY      ; Local display procedure
              JMP     MONITOR
;
;****************|
;  exit to MS-DOS |
;****************|
DOS_EXIT:
              MOV     AH,76           ; DOS service request number
              MOV     AL,0            ; No return code
              INT     21H             ; Exit to DOS
;***************************************************************
;                       procedures
;***************************************************************
;
DOS_DISPLAY     PROC    NEAR
; Display a formatted text string using DOS service number 9 of
; interrupt 21H
; On entry:
;          DX -> string terminated in $ sign
```

```
; On exit:
;         string is displayed at the current cursor position
        MOV     AH,9            ; Service request
        INT     21H             ; MS-DOS service interrupt
        RET
DOS_DISPLAY     ENDP
;**************************************************************
;
SERIAL_TTY      PROC    NEAR
; Display character or control code at cursor position
; using BIOS teletype service number 14 of interrupt 10H
; Add a line feed code (0AH) if the character was a carriage
; return (0DH)
TTY_ONE:
        PUSH    AX              ; Save character
        MOV     AH,14           ; BIOS service request number
                                ; for ASCII teletype write
        MOV     BX,0            ; Display page
        INT     10H             ; BIOS service request
        POP     AX
; Test for carriage return and add line feed
        CMP     AL,0DH
        JNE     NOT_CR
        MOV     AL,0AH
        JMP     TTY_ONE
NOT_CR:
        RET
SERIAL_TTY      ENDP
;**************************************************************
;
GET_KEY         PROC    NEAR
; Read keyboard character
        MOV     AH,0            ; BIOS service request number
        INT     16H
        RET
GET_KEY         ENDP
;**************************************************************
;
CODE    ENDS
        END     ENTRY_POINT     ; Reference to label at which
                                ; execution starts
```

VOCABULARY

asynchronous	intelligent device
asynchronous communications adapter	jumpers
baud rate	null modem
character bit	parity bit
communications protocol	RS-232-C
data set ready	serial/parallel adapter
data terminal ready	serial port
dumb terminal	start bit
handshaking	software handshaking
hardware handshaking	transmitter holding register

QUESTIONS

1. What is the main difference between serial and parallel communications?
2. How are the serial ports designated in MS-DOS?
3. What is RS-232-C?
4. What element in the transmission does the baud rate measure?
5. List the three possible parity settings in the IBM microcomputers?
6. Can an IBM microcomputer be equipped with more than one serial port?
7. What does DTR and DSR stand for?
8. What is the XON/XOFF protocol?
9. What is a D-shell connector?
10. How are the transmit and receive lines connected in null modem wiring?
11. What BIOS interrupt provides serial communications services?
12. In what location of the BIOS data area can we find the base address of the first serial port?

EXERCISES

1. Draw a flowchart for the poll, send, and display routine starting a text reference # 5 in the program LESSON9.ASM.
2. Modify the LESSON9.ASM program so that data read operations are performed by using direct access to the serial port.
3. Design and code a terminal program similar to LESSON9.ASM but with two user-selectable modes: one to receive and one to send data.

10

Disk Operations

10.0 DATA STORAGE

The primary storage in a computer system, usually called *random access memory* (*RAM*), is a volatile and expensive medium. Most computer systems, including the IBM micro-computers, also contain a permanent, nonvolatile form of memory called *read only memory* (*ROM*). Computers, small or large, usually require some form of auxiliary storage as an alternative data storage facility. In mainframe computers auxiliary storage devices started with the punched card and punched tape technology. In the IBM microcomputers the first auxiliary storage devices, and still today the most used, are based on magnetic data encoding technology.

Auxiliary storage usually serves as an extension of the system's main memory. Programs and data can be temporarily stored in an auxiliary device but must be moved to main memory for execution or manipulation by the software. In this sense auxiliary storage devices serve as a relatively inexpensive, nonvolatile, information storage medium, but not as a substitute for main memory. However, it is possible that this concept will have to be revised in the near future as data storage devices become more flexible and efficient.

As previously mentioned, in the IBM microcomputers the system's main memory is composed of ROM and RAM. Auxiliary storage devices are based almost exclusively on magnetic and optical technology. Magnetic storage devices are classified into two groups according to how data are stored and retrieved. Devices that can access an individual data item are said to be of *direct access* type. Devices in which data are stored linearly, so that it is necessary to cross over other stored data in order to reach the desired item, are classified in the *sequential access* type. The disk or diskette system is a direct access device, whereas a magnetic tape recording is a sequential access device. Optical drives are usually considered direct access devices.

172

Disk and Diskette Storage

The most popular medium for microcomputer data storage consists of a thin, polyester disk coated with a metal oxide similar to the one used in magnetic tapes. In the IBM microcomputers these magnetic disks can be of 5 1/4" or 3 1/2" diameter. The 5 1/4" type, usually called a diskette or floppy disk, is used in all models of the PC line except the PC convertible. The 3 1/2" type, called a microdisk, is used in the PC convertible and in all models of the PS/2 line.

A fixed disk is a nonremovable internal storage device that uses metal disks coated with a magnetic substance similar to that used in diskettes and microdisks. Many IBM microcomputers are equipped with fixed disks. Data are recorded on the magnetic surface of a diskette, microdisk, or fixed disk in a pattern of concentric circles called *tracks*. Each track is divided into areas called *sectors*. The read-write head is moved from track to track by a stepper motor while the storage media spins on its axis. In the course of this chapter we will use the word "disk" when referring to either diskettes, microdisks, or fixed disk media or devices.

10.1 DATA STORAGE IN MS-DOS

In the IBM microcomputers the management and programming of disk devices are left almost entirely to the operating system software. Table 10.1 shows the diskette and microdisk storage formats.

TABLE 10.1 DISKETTE AND MICRODISK FORMATS IN IBM MICROCOMPUTERS

STORAGE MEDIA	SIDES	TRACKS	SECTORS	TRACKS PER INCH	CAPACITY	DOS
5¼" diskette	1	40	8	48	160Kb	1.1
	1	40	9	48	180Kb	1.2 +
	2	40	8	48	320Kb	2.0
	2	40	9	48	360Kb	2.0 +
	2	80	15	96	1.2Mb	3.0 +
3½" microdisk	2	80	9	135	720Kb	3.0 +
	2	80	18	135	1.4Mb	3.0 +

Physical Elements of Magnetic Storage

In the original version of the Personal Computer, operating under MS-DOS version 1.1 and 1.2, the diskette drive was equipped with a single read-write head. In this design one side of the diskette is used to store data (see Table 10.1). MS-DOS version 2.0 first introduced the double-sided drives, which quickly became the standard. The track density has gone from 48 tracks per inch in the drives of the PC line (double density), 96 tracks per inch in the PC AT (quad density), and 135 tracks per inch in the 3 1/2" microdisks of the PC convertible and the PS/2 line. The amount of data recorded in each diskette sector is 512 bytes for all fixed disk and diskette systems.

In a magnetic disk storage system data are recorded in concentric circles on the disk's surface. These circles are named tracks in diskette and microdisk technology and cylinders in fixed disk storage. Each track or cylinder is further divided into areas called sectors. Figure 10.1 shows the structure of tracks and sectors on a magnetic disk.

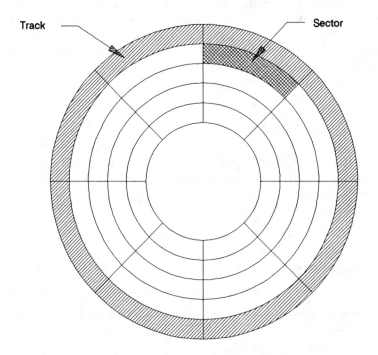

Figure 10.1 Magnetic Storage Structure

MS-DOS Logical Structures

MS-DOS uses several logical structures to manage the storage and retrieval of magnetic data. The following are the most important of these structures.

The *file allocation table* (FAT) is a control structure that maps the available storage space and keeps an inventory of the tracks that are used, unused, or damaged.

The *disk directory* provides a formatted list of the name, attributes, times of creation and update, and size of the files and subdirectories on the storage media.

The *disk transfer area* (DTA) is an area of RAM used by MS-DOS to store data during certain disk operations. A default DTA is provided by MS-DOS during program load; however, applications usually change the DTA to their own memory space.

The *file control block* (FCB) is a formatted data structure located in RAM and used by MS-DOS to temporarily store file information. This structure was originally designed for compatibility with the CP/M operating system. Traditional MS-DOS functions require that the programmer initialize and prepare the FCB in order to perform file operations. MS-DOS version 2.0 introduced the use of *file handles*; which simplify programming disk operations.

File Handles

All of the MS-DOS logical structures mentioned above contain data that may be of occasional interest to the programmer. However, with the introduction of file handles (in MS-DOS version 2.0) it is possible to perform disk operations without accessing the system's control areas directly. The handle-type services should, in general, be preferred over the traditional FCB-type services due to their greater efficiency and programming ease. The program named LESSON10.ASM, listed at the end of this chapter, performs several disk operations using MS-DOS handle-type services.

The file handle is a word-size constant that MS-DOS assigns to a file or device. The concept of identification codes associated with files originated in the UNIX operating system, where they are called *file descriptors*. Several character devices have predefined handles in MS-DOS; these are listed in Table 10.2.

TABLE 10.2 FILE HANDLES FOR MS-DOS CHARACTER DEVICES

DEVICE NAME	MS-DOS DESIGNATION	HANDLE
Standard input	CON	0
Standard output	CON	1
Standard error	CON	2
Auxiliary	AUX	3
List device	PRN	4

Disk files are assigned handles using MS-DOS services of interrupt 21H. Once a file is assigned a handle the program can use it in any subsequent reference to this file.

10.2 PROGRAMMING DISK OPERATIONS

Like so many other devices in the IBM microcomputers, disk operations can be programmed at three different levels: using BIOS services, using MS-DOS services, or accessing the disk hardware directly. The services provided in the BIOS perform very elementary operations that would be of interest mainly to programmers requiring primitive disk functions. This is also the case regarding direct access to the video hardware. MS-DOS disk services, on the other hand, provide an extensive selection of disk functions that accommodate most practical needs. The following MS-DOS disk services are particularly useful.

1. MS-DOS service number 14, interrupt 21H is used to set the default disk drive. The zero-based value is passed in the DL register as follows: DL = 0 for drive A, DL = 1 for drive B, and so on.

2. MS-DOS service number 23, interrupt 21H is used to rename a disk file. Its use is shown in the following code fragment:

```
DATA      SEGMENT
;
DOS_BUFFER        DB      0                 ; Default drive
                  DB      'OLDFNAME'        ; 8-character field
                  DB      '111'             ; 3-character field
                  DB      5 DUP (00H)       ; Required by DOS
                  DB      'NEWFNAME'        ; 8-character field
                  DB      '222'             ; 3-character field
                  DB      15 DUP (00H)      ; Required by DOS
DATA      ENDS
;
CODE      SEGMENT
          .
          .
          .
; Code to rename the file OLDFNAME.111 as NEWFNAME.222
          MOV     AH,23             ; DOS Service Request number
          LEA     DX,DOS_BUFFER     ; Pointer to buffer
          INT     21H               ; MS-DOS interrupt
          .
          .
```

3. MS-DOS service number 26, interrupt 21H is used to set the disk transfer area to the program's data space. The use of this services is shown in the SET_DTA procedure of the program LESSON10.ASM.

4. MS-DOS service number 60, interrupt 21H is used to create a file and obtain the file handle. The use of this service is shown in the OPEN_CREATE procedure in the program LESSON10.ASM.

5. MS-DOS service number 61, interrupt 21H is used to open an existing file and obtain its file handle. The use of this service is shown in the OPEN_CREATE procedure in the program LESSON10.ASM.

6. MS-DOS service number 62, interrupt 21H is used to close an open file using the file's handle. The use of this service is shown in the CLOSE_FILE procedure in the program LESSON10.ASM.

7. MS-DOS service number 63, interrupt 21H is used to read data from an open file, using the file's handle, and transfer these data to a buffer designated by the caller. The use of this service is shown in the READ_128 procedure in the program LESSON10.ASM.

8. MS-DOS service number 64, interrupt 21H is used to write data to an open file from a buffer designated by the caller. The service uses the file's handle. With every call to this service the file pointer is automatically updated to point to the next sector. The BX register is used to pass the file handle to the service. CX holds the number of bytes to write, and DS:DX points to the address of the buffer holding the data to be written.

10.3 ELEMENTS OF THE PROGRAM LESSON10.ASM

The program LESSON10.ASM obtains a path or filename designation from the user and searches the storage system for a matching file. If a match is found, the file is opened and its contents are read into a buffer and displayed on the screen. The read and display operation is performed 128 bytes at a time. Control characters with a value smaller than 0AH are not displayed. When the end of the file is reached, the file is closed and control returns to MS-DOS. If the program fails to find a matching path or filename, an error message is displayed and execution is terminated. Figure 10.2 is a flowchart of the program.

Set the Disk Transfer Area

The program LESSON10.ASM begins by setting the disk transfer area (DTA) to a buffer located in its own memory space (see text reference # 1). This operation is necessary so that file data can be conveniently accessed by the code.

Open a Disk File and Obtain Handle

The code proceeds to obtain from the user the path or filename (see text reference # 2) by means of the procedure named OPEN_CREATE (text reference # 3). As its name indicates, this procedure can be used to open an existing file or to create a new file. Which operation is performed depends on a code passed in the BL register (text reference # 4). The procedure uses MS-DOS service number 10 of interrupt 21H to obtain a string of keyboard characters representing the path or filename (see text reference # 5). The buffer format is also shown in the data segment under text reference # 6.

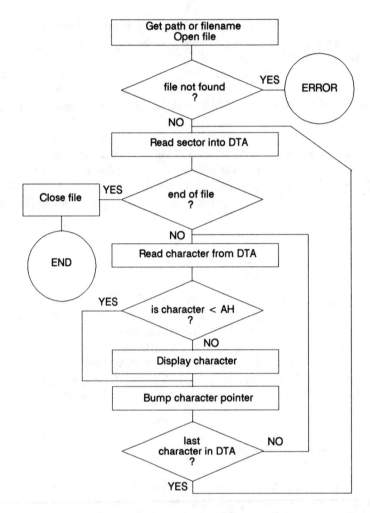

Figure 10.2 Flowchart for LESSON10.ASM

The procedure OPEN_CREATE is used by the LESSON10.ASM program to open an existing file. If the path or filename is found, then the file's handle is returned in AX. The program stores this handle for future reference in a memory variable (see text reference # 7).

Coding an Error Handler

Because the pathname or filename typed by the user can contain invalid data or reference nonexisting drives, directories, or filenames, the program must take into account the possibility of failure of the OPEN_CREATE procedure. For this reason the code examines the carry flag returned by OPEN_CREATE (see text reference # 8). If the flag is set, indicating that the open operation failed, the program displays an error message and aborts execution.

Read Data from a Disk File

If the file was successfully opened, the program uses the file handle (stored in a local variable) to read and display the file's contents (see text reference # 9). The actual read operation is performed in 128-byte sectors by the procedure named READ_128. The program examines the contents of the AX register after each call to READ_128 to see if the end of the file was reached (see text reference # 11). If the file pointer is not at the end of the file, then the contents of the disk transfer area are displayed on the screen one byte at a time. Control codes with a value smaller than 0AH are bypassed by the display routine (see text reference # 12). This is done to avoid confusing actions produced by codes like the backspace (08H) and bell (07H) as interpreted by the BIOS teletype service. This logic is shown in the flowchart of Figure 10.2.

Close a Disk File

When the end of the file is reached during the read operation, the program closes the open file using its handle. This is performed by the CLOSE_FILE procedure (see text reference # 13.)

10.4 SOURCE CODE LISTING OF THE PROGRAM LESSON10.ASM

```
;****************************************************************
;****************************************************************
;                         LESSON10.ASM
;****************************************************************
;****************************************************************
; Program title: LESSON10
; Start date:
; Last modification:
;
; Program description:
; Request a path and filename from the user, open the specified
; disk file, and display its contents
;
; New operations:
; 1. Set the disk transfer area (DTA) to the program's memory
```

```
;    space
; 2. Open a disk file and obtain the file handle
; 3. Handle errors returned by an MS-DOS service
; 4. Read data from a disk file into a buffer
; 5. Close a disk file using its handle
;
;*******************************************************************
;                          stack segment
;*******************************************************************
STACK     SEGMENT stack
;
                   DB        1024 DUP ('?')   ; Default stack is 1K
STACK     ENDS
;
;*******************************************************************
;                          data segment
;*******************************************************************
DATA      SEGMENT
;
;********************|
; text message strings |
;********************|
INPUT_MSG       DB        'Enter path or filename: $'
NO_HANDLE       DB        0AH,0DH,'ERROR - file not opened'
                DB        0AH,0DH,'$'
;********************|
;    pathname buffer   |
;      and data        |
;********************|
;                                    |********************|
;                                    | text reference # 6 |
;                                    |********************|
; Buffer formatted for MS-DOS service number 10, interrupt 21H
; to read a string of keyboard characters
PATH_BUFFER     DB        28       ; Maximum characters allowed
                DB        0        ; Characters actually entered
PATH_NAME       DB        30 DUP (00H)    ; Buffer storage area
;
FILE_HANDLE     DW        0        ; Storage for file handle
;********************|
; disk transfer area   |
;********************|
```

```
LOCAL_DTA        DB       128 DUP (00H)   ; Program's disk transfer
                                          ; area
DATA    ENDS
;****************************************************************
;                          code segment
;****************************************************************
;
CODE    SEGMENT
        ASSUME  CS:CODE
;*********************|
;    initialization   |
;*********************|
ENTRY_POINT:
; Initialize the DATA segment so that the program can access the
; stored data items using the DS segment register
        MOV     AX,DATA          ; Address of DATA to AX
        MOV     DS,AX            ; and to DS
        ASSUME  DS:DATA          ; Assume directive so that
                                 ; the assembler defaults to DS
;                                       |*********************|
;                                       | text reference # 1 |
;                                       |*********************|
;*********************|
;     set DTA         |
;*********************|
; Set the system's disk transfer area to the program's data
; space
        LEA     DX,LOCAL_DTA     ; Pointer to program's DTA
        CALL    SET_DTA          ; Local procedure
;*********************|
;  clear screen and   |
;   display message   |
;*********************|
        CALL    CLEAR_SCREEN     ; Local procedure
; Set cursor at bottom screen row
        MOV     DL,0             ; First column
        MOV     DH,24            ; Last row
        CALL    SET_CURSOR       ; Local procedure
;                                       |*********************|
;                                       | text reference # 2 |
;                                       |*********************|
; Display entry message
```

```
            LEA       DX,INPUT_MSG     ; Pointer to message string
            CALL      DOS_DISPLAY      ; Local procedure
;**********************|
;    open file and     |
;      get handle      |
;**********************|
            MOV       BL,0             ; Code for open file function
            LEA       DX,PATH_BUFFER   ; Pointer to buffer area
            CALL      OPEN_CREATE      ; Local procedure
;                                      |********************|
;                                      | text reference # 8 |
;                                      |********************|
; At this point the carry flag is set if the open operation
; failed
            JNC       FILE_OK          ; Go if no carry
;**********************|
;  ERROR - file not    |
;          opened      |
;**********************|
; Display error message and exit
            LEA       DX,NO_HANDLE     ; Pointer to error message
            CALL      DOS_DISPLAY      ; Local procedure
            JMP       DOS_EXIT         ; End execution
;                                      |********************|
;                                      | text reference # 9 |
;                                      |********************|
;**********************|
;    file opened       |
;**********************|
; At this point the file was successfully opened and the AX
; register holds the file handle
FILE_OK:
;                                      |********************|
;                                      | text reference # 7 |
;                                      |********************|
            MOV       FILE_HANDLE,AX   ; Store handle in variable
;**********************|
;    read 1 sector     |
;**********************|
NEW_SECTOR:
            MOV       BX,FILE_HANDLE   ; Handle from open function
            LEA       DX,LOCAL_DTA     ; 128-byte buffer area
```

```
        CALL    READ_128        ; Local procedure
; AX holds the number of bytes read into the buffer
;                                |*********************|
;                                | text reference # 11 |
;                                |*********************|
; AX = 0 if read operation found the end of file
        CMP     AX,0            ; Test for end of file
        JNE     NOT_EOF         ; Go if not at end
;*********************|
;  end of file exit   |
;*********************|
; At this point the end of the file was reached. Program must
; close the file and end execution
        MOV     BX,FILE_HANDLE  ; Handle from open operation
        CALL    CLOSE_FILE      ; Local procedure
        JMP     DOS_EXIT
;*********************|
;   display file data |
;*********************|
NOT_EOF:
        MOV     CX,AX           ; CX counts number of bytes
                                ; to display
        LEA     SI,LOCAL_DTA    ; Pointer to buffer area
                                ; holding disk data
DISPLAY_DATA:
        MOV     AL,[SI]         ; Get buffer byte
;                                |*********************|
;                                | text reference # 12 |
;                                |*********************|
; Test for invalid codes < 0AH
        CMP     AL,0AH          ; Less than 10H are control codes
        JB      IS_CONTROL      ; Go if character < 10H
        PUSH    CX              ; Save byte counter
        PUSH    SI              ; Save buffer point
        CALL    TTY             ; Local procedure
        POP     SI              ; Restore registers
        POP     CX
IS_CONTROL:
        INC     SI              ; Bump buffer pointer
        LOOP    DISPLAY_DATA
; At this point the data in the buffers has been displayed
        JMP     NEW_SECTOR
```

```
;*********************|
;    exit to MS-DOS   |
;*********************|
DOS_EXIT:
        MOV     AH,76           ; DOS service request number
        MOV     AL,0            ; No return code
        INT     21H             ; Exit to DOS
;****************************************************************
;                          procedures
;****************************************************************
TTY     PROC    NEAR
; Local procedure to display a character using BIOS teletype
; service number 14 of INT 10H
        PUSH    AX              ; Save AX in stack
        MOV     AH,14           ; Service request number
        MOV     BX,0            ; Display page is usually 0
        INT     10H             ; BIOS video service interrupt
        POP     AX              ; Restore AX from stack
        RET                     ; End of procedure
TTY     ENDP
;****************************************************************
CLEAR_SCREEN    PROC    NEAR
; Clear the video display using BIOS service number 6 of
; interrupt 10H
; On entry:
;           Nothing
        MOV     AH,06           ; Service request
        MOV     AL,0            ; Code to blank entire window
        MOV     BH,07           ; Use normal attribute
        MOV     CX,0            ; Start at row 0, column 0
        MOV     DH,24           ; End at row 24
        MOV     DL,79           ; Column 79
        INT     10H             ; BIOS video service
        RET
CLEAR_SCREEN    ENDP
;****************************************************************
;
DOS_DISPLAY     PROC    NEAR
; Display a formatted text string using DOS service number 9 of
; interrupt 21H
; On entry:
;           DX -> string terminated in $ sign
```

```
; On exit:
;           string is displayed at the current cursor position
          MOV     AH,9            ; Service request
          INT     21H             ; MS-DOS service interrupt
          RET
DOS_DISPLAY     ENDP
;*****************************************************************
;
SET_CURSOR      PROC    NEAR
; Procedure to set the system cursor using BIOS service number 2
; of interrupt 10H. The program assumes that a text mode is
; active and that the text screen contains 80 columns by 25 rows
; On entry:
;           DH = desired cursor row (range 0 to 24)
;           DL = desired cursor column (0 to 79)
; On exit:
;           System cursor positioned
;
          PUSH    AX              ; Save AX register
          MOV     BH,0            ; Display page 0
          MOV     AH,02           ; BIOS service request number
          INT     10H             ; Interrupt for BIOS service
          POP     AX              ; Restore AX
          RET
SET_CURSOR      ENDP
;
;*****************************************************************
;                    disk operations procedures
;*****************************************************************
SET_DTA         PROC    NEAR
; Set memory area to be used by DOS as disk transfer area
; On entry:
;           DX -> 128-bytes buffer to be used as DTA
;
; On exit:
;           carry clear
;
          MOV     AH,26           ; DOS service request
          INT     21H
          RET
SET_DTA         ENDP
;*****************************************************************
```

```
;                                            |*********************|
;                                            | text reference # 3 |
;                                            |*********************|
;
OPEN_CREATE        PROC        NEAR
;
; Use DOS buffered keyboard input service to input a filename,
; to open file, and to return a 16-bit file handle that can be
; used to access the file
; The routine's action depends on the setting of the BL register
; On entry:
;                                            |*********************|
;                                            | text reference # 5 |
;                                            |*********************|
;         DX -> Buffer formatted as for DOS service number 10
;                    Offset 0 = maximum characters to input
;                    Offset 1 = characters actually input,
;                                     excluding CR
;                                            |*********************|
;                                            | text reference # 4 |
;                                            |*********************|
;         BL = 0 - Open file
;         BL = 1 - Create new file
; On exit:
;         carry clear if file open - operation successful
;           AX = 16-bit file handle
;         carry set if operation failed
;           AX = error code as follows:
;                1 = invalid function
;                2 = file not found
;
; Note: This procedure assumes that DOS service number 26
;       has been previously used to set the DTA address
;
;****************|
; buffered input |
; from keyboard  |
;****************|
        PUSH     BX                 ; Save exit/create switch
        MOV      AH,10              ; DOS service request number
        PUSH     DX                 ; Save buffer start address
        PUSH     DX                 ; twice
```

```
            INT     21H                 ; To DOS
; Filename now in buffer. Set a null byte in buffer to
; create an ASCIIZ string for the PATH or FILENAME
            POP     DI                  ; Recover buffer start
            INC     DI                  ; To input count byte
            MOV     AL,[DI]             ; No. of characters in buffer
            MOV     AH,0                ; Prepare for addition
            ADD     DI,AX               ; DX -> CR byte
            INC     DI                  ; One more
            MOV     BYTE PTR [DI],0H
                                        ; Set null byte terminator
; Recover buffer address and open/create switch
            POP     DX                  ; Buffer start
            ADD     DX,2                ; Index to path or filename
            POP     BX                  ; Open/create switch
            CMP     BL,0                ; Test for open switch
            JE      OPEN_F
            JMP     CREATE_F
;*****************|
;       open      |
;*****************|
OPEN_F:
; This routine opens a file for read/write access if the filename
; is contained in the form of an ASCIIZ string pointed by DX
            MOV     AH,61               ; DOS service request number
                                        ; to open file (handle mode)
            MOV     AL,2                ; Read/write access
            INT     21H
; Carry set if open failed
; If carry clear, file is open and AX = file handle
; BL (in stack) holds exit/create switch
            RET
;*****************|
;      create     |
;*****************|
CREATE_F:
            MOV     CX,0                ; Normal access
            MOV     AH,60               ; DOS service request
            INT     21H
; If carry clear, AX = handle for new file
; If carry set, create function failed
            RET
```

```
OPEN_CREATE   ENDP
;****************************************************************
;                                              |********************|
;                                              | text reference # 13 |
;                                              |********************|
CLOSE_FILE      PROC    NEAR
; Close file using file handle
; On entry:
;           BX = file handle
; On exit:
;           carry clear if operation successful - file closed
;           carry set if operation failed - invalid handle or file
;           not open
;
        MOV     AH,62           ; DOS service request
        INT     21H
        RET
CLOSE_FILE      ENDP
;****************************************************************
;                                              |********************|
;                                              | text reference # 10 |
;                                              |********************|
READ_128        PROC    NEAR
; Read 128 bytes from an open file into buffer using the file
; handle. This procedure assumes that the file has been
; previously opened or created using the procedure OPEN_CREATE
;
; On entry:
;           BX =   file handle
;           DX -> 128 bytes user buffer
; On exit:
;           carry clear if operation successful
;             AX = number of bytes read into buffer
;             AX = 0 if end of file
;           carry set if operation failed
;             AX = error code
;                  5 = access denied
;                  6 = invalid handle or file not open
;
        PUSH    CX              ; Save entry CX
        MOV     AH,63           ; DOS service request
        MOV     CX,128          ; Bytes to read
```

```
            INT      21H
            POP      CX              ; Restore
            RET
READ_128             ENDP
;***************************************************************
CODE        ENDS
            END      ENTRY_POINT     ; Reference to label at which
                                     ; execution starts
```

VOCABULARY

direct access   file handles
disk directory   random access memory
disk transfer area   read only memory
file allocation table   sectors
file control block   sequential access
file descriptors   tracks

QUESTIONS

1. What words are uased in forming the acronyms "RAM" and "ROM"?
2. What is the difference between direct access and sequential access?
3. What is the name of a nonremovable magenetic storage device used in the IBM microcomputers?
4. What type of storage device is usually called a microdisk?
5. What are tracks and sectors in magenetic storage?
6. Can an application change the location of the disk transfer area?
7. What is the MS-DOS structure that holds the names and other information of existing files?
8. What is a file handle?
9. What is the number of the file handle for the keyboard (standard input) device?
10. What MS-DOS service can be used to close a file using the file handle?

EXERCISES

1. Design and code a program that reads the contents of a disk file and sends the ASCII characters in the range 20H to F7H to a parallel printer.
2. Design and code a program that reads a disk file and displays its contents in two separate screen areas. One area contains the ASCII and extended char-

acters (range 20H to FFH). The second area contains the numerical values of
the control codes and symbols smaller than 20H.
3. Design and code a communications program with two modes. In the first mode
the program opens a disk file and transmits its contents through the serial port.
In the second mode the program receives data through the serial port and
saves them in a disk file. Provide the necessary handshake signals to transmit
and receive the filename, the start and end of a sector, and the end of the file.

Appendix A

Most Used BIOS Services

BIOS INTERRUPT 10H — VIDEO SERVICES

SERVICE NUMBER	ON ENTRY	ON EXIT	DESCRIPTION
0	AL	Nothing	Set video mode (in AL)
1	CX	Nothing	Set cursor type

```
0  1  2  4  3  2  1  0 CL bits
└──┴──┘  └──┴──┴──┘
   │           └──────────────── Top cursor line
   └────────────────────────── RESERVED (must be 0)

0  1  2  4  3  2  1  0 CH bits
└──┴──┘  └──┴──┴──┘
   │           └──────────────── Bottom cursor line
   └────────────────────────── RESERVED (must be 0)
```

SERVICE NUMBER	ON ENTRY	ON EXIT	DESCRIPTION
2	DX-BH	Nothing	Set cursor position DH = row number (0-based) DL = column number (0-based) BH = page number (0-based)
3	BH	CX-DX	Read cursor position BH = page number (0-based) Returns: DH = current cursor row (0-based) DL = current cursor column (0-based) CH = cursor start line CL = cursor end line
4	Nothing	AH-CH-BX DX	Read light pen position Returns: AH = 01 if valid value in registers CH = light pen pixel row (0 to 199) BX = light pen pixel column (0 to 639) DH = character row (0 to 24) DL = character column (0 to 79) Note: The light pen function is not available in the PC Convertible and the PS/2 line.

(continued)

BIOS INTERRUPT 10H — VIDEO SERVICES (continued)

SERVICE NUMBER	ON ENTRY	ON EXIT	DESCRIPTION
5	AL	Nothing	Select display page (except PCjr) AL = page number
6	AL-BH-CX DX	Nothing	Scroll page up or initialize AL = number of lines to scroll AL = 0 to initialize window BH = attribute for initialization CH/CL = row/column of upper left corner of window DH/DL = row/column of lower right corner of window
7	AL-BH-CX DX	Nothing	Scroll page down or initialize AL = number of lines to scroll AL = 0 to initialize window BH = attribute for initialization CH/CL = row/column of upper left corner of window DH/DL = row/column of lower right corner of window
8	BH	AX	Read character and attribute at present cursor position BH = page number (0-based) Returns: AL = character AH = attribute
9	AL-BX-CX	Nothing	Write character and attribute at current cursor position AL = character to write (in ASCII) BL = attribute (character color in graphics modes) BH = display page (0-based) CX = count of characters to repeat Note: The repeat count (in CX) is valid only for the same row. This function can be used to display text while in a graphics mode.
10	AL-BH-CX	Nothing	Write character at current cursor position (no attribute) AL = character to write (in ASCII) BH = display page (0-based) CX = count of characters to repeat Note: The repeat count (in CX) is valid only for the same row.
11	BX	Nothing	Set color palette in CGA systems (See also service number 16) BH = color ID (0 or 1) If BH = 0, set background color for 320 x 200 graphics modes or border color in alpha modes. Set foreground color in 640 x 200 graphics modes. BL must be in the range 0 to 31. BL = color value
12	AL-CX-DX	Nothing	Write pixel in graphics modes AL = pixel color requested If bit 7 of AL is set, then color is XORed with pixel contents. CX = pixel column DX = pixel row

(continued)

BIOS INTERRUPT 10H — VIDEO SERVICES (continued)

SERVICE NUMBER	ON ENTRY	ON EXIT	DESCRIPTION
13	CX-DX	AL	Read pixel in graphics modes CX = pixel column DX = pixel row Returns: AL = color value of pixel read
14	AL-BX	Nothing	Write character in teletype mode (at current cursor position) AL = character code in ASCII BH = display page BL = foreground color in graphics modes Note: Carriage return (0DH), line feed (0AH), backspace (08H), and bell (07H) codes are intepreted as commands. Line wrapping and screen scrolling are provided.
15	Nothing	AX-BH	Get current video mode Returns: AL = active mode AH = number of screen columns BH = active video page (0 based)

16	AL-BL
	ES:DX
		ES:DX	Set color palette
			(EGA/VGA BIOS extension)
			
			PCjr, EGA, AND PS/2 SYSTEMS
			AL = 0 to set individual palette registers
			    BL = register to set BH = color value
			AL = 1 to set overscan register (border color)
			    BH = color value
			AL = 2 to set palette and overscan registers
			    ES:DX -> 17-byte table:
			    bytes 0–15 = palette register values
			    byte 16 = border color value
			AL = 3 to toggle intensity and blinking attribute
			    BL = 0 to enable intensity
			    BL = 1 to enable blinking

BIOS INTERRUPT 11H — EQUIPMENT DETERMINATION

SERVICE NUMBER	ON ENTRY	ON EXIT	DESCRIPTION
Not Required	Nothing	AX	Return system devices as in BIOS data area 0040:0010 (see Table 9.5)

Returns:
AX = equipment flags as follows
15 14 13 12 11 10 9 8 AH bit map

———— RESERVED
———— No. of RS-232C adapters
———— RESERVED
———— Internal modem (in PC Convertible only)
———— Number of printer adapters

7 6 5 4 3 2 1 0 AL bit map

———— IPL diskette installed
———— Math coprocessor installed
———— PS/2 pointing device
———— RESERVED in PC line
———— RESERVED
Video hardware:
00 = RESERVED
01 = 40 x 25 color
10 = 80 x 25 color
11 = 80 x 25 monochrome
Diskette drives (if bit 0 = 1):
00 = 1 drive
01 = 2 drives
10 = 3 drives
11 = 4 drives

BIOS INTERRUPT 14H — SERIAL PORT FUNCTIONS

SERVICE NUMBER	ON ENTRY	ON EXIT	DESCRIPTION
0	AL-DX	AX	Initialize serial port

AL = initialization parameters

```
7  6  5  4  3  2  1  0   AL bit map
└──┘     └──┘     └──┘
```

Word length:
10 = 7 bits
11 = 8 bits

Stop bits:
0 = 1 stop bit
1 = 2 stop bits

Parity:
00 = no parity   01 = odd parity
10 = no parity   11 = even parity

Baud rate:
000 = 110 Bd   001 = 150 Bd
101 = 300 Bd   011 = 600 Bd
100 = 1200 Bd   101 = 2400 Bd
110 = 4800 Bd   111 = 9600 Bd

DX = communications port (range 0 to 3)

Returns:

AH = serial port status

```
7  6  5  4  3  2  1  0   AH bit map
```

Data ready
Overrun error
Parity error
Framing error
Break error
Transmitter holding register empty
Transmitter shift register empty
Time-out (if this bit is set, all
other bits are not significant

AL = modem status

```
7  6  5  4  3  2  1  0   AL bit map
```

Change in clear to send
Change in data set ready
Trailing edge ring indicator
Change in receive line signal
Clear to send
Data set ready
Ring indicator
Received line signal detected

| 1 | AL-DX | AX | Send character |

AL = character to send
DX = communications port (range 0 to 3)
Returns:
    AH = line status (see service number 0)
    AL is preserved

(continued)

BIOS INTERRUPT 14H — SERIAL PORT FUNCTIONS (Continued)

SERVICE NUMBER	ON ENTRY	ON EXIT	DESCRIPTION

2	DX	AX	Receive character
			
			DX = communications port (range 0 to 3)
			Returns:
			    AL = character received
			    AH = line status (see service number 0)
			Note: This service waits for a character.

3	DX	AX	Read status
			
			DX = communications port (range 0 to 3)
			Returns:
			    AL = modem status (see service number 0)
			    AH = line status (see service number 0)

BIOS INTERRUPT 16H — KEYBOARD FUNCTIONS

SERVICE NUMBER	ON ENTRY	ON EXIT	DESCRIPTION

0	Nothing	AX	Read keyboard (wait for key)
			
			Returns:
			  AL = ASCII character code
			  AH = scan code
			Note: This service waits for a keystroke to become available.

1	Nothing	AX-zf	Return keyboard status
			
			Returns:
			  Zero flag set (zf = 1) if no code available
			  Zero flag clear (zf = 0) if code available
			  AL = ASCII character code
			  AH = scan code

2	Nothing	AL	Return keyboard flags
			
			Returns:
			  AL = keyboard flags
			  7 6 5 4 3 2 1 0 AL bit map
			    1 = right shift key pressed
			    1 = left shift key pressed
			    1 = Ctrl key pressed
			    1 = Alt key pressed
			    1 = Scroll Lock locked
			    1 = Num Lock locked
			    1 = Caps Lock locked
			    1 = Insert key locked
			  AH = RESERVED

3	AL-BX	Nothing	Set typematic rate
			
			PC AT BIOS dated 11/15/85 and later, PC XT Model 286, and PS/2 SYSTEMS
			AL = 5 to set typematic rate and delay
			BL = typematic rate in characters per second (cps)
			  0 = 30.0 cps 1 = 26.7 cps 2 = 24.0 cps
			  3 = 21.8 cps 4 = 20.0 cps 5 = 18.5 cps
			  6 = 17.1 cps 7 = 16.0 cps 8 = 15.0 cps
			  9 = 13.3 cps 10 = 12.0 cps 11 = 10.9 cps
			  12 = 10.0 cps 13 = 9.2 cps 14 = 8.6 cps
			  15 = 8.0 cps 16 = 7.5 cps 17 = 6.7 cps
			  18 = 6.0 cps 19 = 5.5 cps 20 = 5.0 cps
			  21 = 4.6 cps 22 = 4.3 cps 23 = 4.0 cps
			  24 = 3.7 cps 25 = 3.3 cps 26 = 3.0 cps
			  27 = 2.7 cps 28 = 2.5 cps 29 = 2.3 cps
			  30 = 2.1 cps 31 = 2.0 cps
			  32 to 255 = RESERVED

4	AL	Nothing	Keyboard click adjustment **PCjr and PC CONVERTIBLE** AL = 0 to set keyboard click OFF AL = 1 to set keyboard click ON

BIOS INTERRUPT 17H — PRINTER FUNCTIONS

SERVICE NUMBER	ON ENTRY	ON EXIT	DESCRIPTION

0	AL-DX	AH	Print character
			
			AL = character to print
			DX = printer port number (0-based)
			Returns:
			    AH = printer status
			
			7 6 5 4 3 2 1 0 AH bit map
			
			                 1 = time-out
			                 RESERVED
			                 RESERVED
			           1 = I/O error
			           1 = printer selected
			       1 = out of paper
			       1 = acknowledge
			       1 = printer not busy

1	DX	AH	Initialize printer DX = printer port number (0-based) Returns: AH = printer status as in service number 0
2	DX	AH	Read printer status DX = printer port number (0-based) Returns: AH = printer status as in service number 0

Appendix B

Most Used Services of MS-DOS Interrupt 21H

MS-DOS INTERRUPT 21H - INPUT AND OUTPUT SERVICES

SERVICE NUMBER	ON ENTRY	ON EXIT	DESCRIPTION
AH = 1		AL	Input keyboard character and echo Operation: Inputs one character from the keyboard and displays it on the video screen. Ctrl C is recognized.
AH = 2	DL		Output to video display Operation: The character in DL is displayed on the video screen. The backspace key (08H) moves the cursor left one position. Ctrl C is recognized.
AH = 3		AL	Input from first serial port Operation: Reads one character from the serial port designated as COM1. Port status not reported.
AH = 4	DL		Output to first serial port Operation: Sends one character to the serial port designated as COM1. Port status not reported.
AH = 5	DL		Output to printer Operation: Sends one character to the printer device designated as PRN or LPT1.

(continued

MS-DOS INTERRUPT 21H - INPUT AND OUTPUT SERVICES (continued)

SERVICE NUMBER	ON ENTRY	ON EXIT	DESCRIPTION
AH = 6	DL	(AL)	Direct input and output DL = 0FFH for input function DL = 0 to FEH for output function Output operation: The character in DL is sent to the standard output device, normally the video display. Input operation: If DL = 0FFH a character is obtained from the standard input device, normally the keyboard. Control codes and system keys are not recognized.
AH = 7		AL	Input keyboard character, no echo, no control codes Operation: Inputs one character from the keyboard. Control codes and system keys are not recognized. The character is not displayed.
AH = 8		AL	Input keyboard character, no echo, control codes recognized Operation: Inputs one character from the keyboard. Control codes and system keys are recognized. The character is not displayed.
AH = 9	DS:DX		Output character string Operation: Displays a text message string terminated in the $ sign. Standard control codes, such as line feed (0AH) and carriage return (0DH) can be embedded in the string.
AH = 10	DS:DX		Input string Operation: Reads a string of characters typed on the keyboard and stores it in a buffer designated by the caller. Buffer must be formatted as follows: OFFSET CONTENTS 0 Maximum character to input. Range is 0 to 255. 1 Number of characters typed by the user before pressing the < Enter > key. The < Enter > keystroke is not counted. 2 Buffer space holding input string Ctrl C and Ctrl Break are active. Control codes are stored preceded by a NULL (00H) byte.

MS-DOS INTERRUPT 21H - DISK SERVICES

SERVICE NUMBER	ON ENTRY	ON EXIT	DESCRIPTION
AH = 14	DL	AL	Set default disk drive Operation: DL holds drive number designation: DL = 0 for drive A DL = 1 for drive B DL = 2 for drive C, an so forth Returns: The number of active drives in AL

AH = 60	CX
	DS:DX
		AX
		cf
			Create a new file using ASCII file specification string
			Operation:
			CX holds file attribute code
			CX = 0 for normal attribute
			CX = 1 for read-only attribute
			CX = 2 for hidden file attribute
			CX = 4 for system file attribute
			DS:DX holds the file specification (pathname or filename) in an ASCII string terminated in a NULL (00H) byte.
			Returns:
			    If carry flag clear AX holds file handle
			    If carry flag set AX holds error code:
			        AX = 3 for path not found
			        AX = 4 for no available file handle
			        AX = 5 for file access denied

AH = 61	CX
	DS:DX
		AX
		cf
			Open an existing file using ASCII file speficification string
			Operation:
			AL bits 0-2 designate the file access mode:
			    000 = read access
			    001 = write access
			    010 = read and write access
			    All other AL bits should be 0
			DS:DX holds the file specification (pathname or filename) in an ASCII string terminated in a NULL (00H) byte.
			Returns:
			    If carry flag clear AX holds file handle
			    If carry flag set AX holds error code:
			    AX = 1 for invalid function
			    AX = 2 and AX = 3 file not found or bad path
			    Other values as in service number 60

AH = 62	BX	AX
		cf
			Close file using file handle
			
			Operation:
			BX holds file handle
			Returns:
			    Carry flag clear if function successful
			    Carry flag set if close operation failed

(continued)

MS-DOS INTERRUPT 21H - DISK SERVICES (continued)

SERVICE NUMBER	ON ENTRY	ON EXIT	DESCRIPTION

AH = 63	BX,CX DS:DX	AX cf	Read open file using handle
			
			Operation:
			This service assumes that the file to be read has been previously created or opened.
			    BX = file handle
			    CX = number of bytes to read
			    DX:DX = address of buffer for data
			    This service updates the file pointer to the last byte read.
			Returns:
			    Carry flag clear if function successful
			    AX = number of bytes read
			    AX = 0 if end of file encountered
			    Carry flag set if read operation failed
			    AX holds error code:
			    AX = 5 for access denied
			    AX = 6 for invalid handle or file not opened

AH = 64	BX,CX DS:DX	AX cf	Write to open file using handle
			
			Operation:
			This service assumes that the file to be written has been previously created or opened.
			    BX = file handle
			    CX = number of bytes to write
			    DX:DX = address of buffer for data
			    This service updates the file pointer to the last byte written.
			Returns:
			    Carry flag clear if function successful
			    AX = number of bytes written
			    AX = 0 if disk full
			    Carry flag set if read operation failed
			    AX holds error code as in service number 63

Appendix C

Basic Set of 80x86 Instructions and Assembler Directives

INSTRUCTIONS AND DIRECTIVES

NAME	I OR D	REFERENCE CHAPTER	DESCRIPTION
ADD	I	Chapter 5	ADDITION Performs the sum of two byte- or word-operands. Both operands must be signed or unsigned binary digits. The sum is found in the destination operand.
AND	I	Chapter 4	LOGICAL AND Performs a logical AND operation of two byte- or word-size operands. A bit in the result is set if both operands are set; otherwise the bit is cleared.
ASSUME	D	Chapter 2	Directive to inform the assembler which named segment to associate with a segment register. This directive affects assembly-time operation and cannot be used as a segment override.
CALL	I	Chapter 3	CALL A PROCEDURE A CALL instruction can refer to a procedure in the same code segment or in a different code segment. Procedures in the same segment are designated NEAR, those in another segment as FAR.

(continued)

INSTRUCTIONS AND DIRECTIVES (coninued)

NAME	I OR D	REFERENCE CHAPTER	D E S C R I P T I O N
CLC	I	Chapter 7	CLEAR CARRY FLAG Zeroes the carry flag.
CLI	I	Chapter 8	CLEAR INTERRUPT FLAG Zeroes the interrupt enable flag so that the 80x86 will not recognize an interrupt request on the INTR line. All maskable interrupts are disabled. Nonmaskable interrupts on the NMI line will be honored.
CMP	I	Chapter 4	COMPARE Subtracts the right operand from the left operand but returns the result only in the flag register. Compare operations are usually followed by a conditional jump.
DB	D	Chapter 2	DEFINE BYTES Assembler directive used to initialize data in one or more byte-size units. An optional variable name can be used to identify the data item at assembly time.
DEC	I		DECREMENT BY 1 Decrements a byte or word operand by one.
DW	D	Chapter 6	DEFINE WORDS Assembler directive used to initialize data in one or more word-size units. An optional variable name can be used to identify the data item at assembly time.
DIV	I	Chapter 7	DIVIDE Divides AX or AX:DX by a byte or word operand. The operation can take the two forms: 1. Byte source AX / source = AL (remainder in AH). 2. Word source AX:DX / source = AX (remainder in DX).
END	D	Chapter 2	END OF SOURCE FILE Directive to inform the assembler of end of a source file. Any statement following this directive is ignored by the assembler. A label operand can be used to identify the location in the source file where execution begins.
ENDS	D	Chapter 2	END OF SEGMENT Assembler directive used with the segment name to mark the end of a program segment.

(continued)

INSTRUCTIONS AND DIRECTIVES (coninued)

NAME	I OR D	REFERENCE CHAPTER	DESCRIPTION
ENDP	D	Chapter 3	END OF PROCEDURE Assembler directive used with the procedure name to mark the end of a procedure.
IN	I	Chapter 9	INPUT (byte or word) Receives a byte or word from the designated port into the AL or AX registers. The port number can be specified as an operand or entered in DX. The latter form allows access to port numbers up to 65,535.
INC	I	Chapter 2	INCREMENT BY 1 The byte or word operand is incremented by 1. If the operand is at the maximum value for the storage unit, the INC instruction will make it wrap-around to 0.
INT	I	Chapter 2	SOFTWARE INTERRUPT Transfers control to a service routine vector located at the interrupt-type times 4. The vector table is located in RAM at 000H to 3FCH and contains 256 entries. The vector stores the destination address in the form OFFSET:SEGMENT.
IRET	I		INTERRUPT RETURN Transfers control to the instruction following the INT xxH instruction. IRET pops IP, CS and the flags from the stack. All flags are affected because they are restored to the values at the time of the interrupt. IRET is normally the last instruction in an interrupt handler.
JA	I		JUMP ON ABOVE Transfers control to the target operand if the destination is larger than the source operand.
JAE JNB JNC	I		JUMP ON ABOVE OR EQUAL Transfers control to the target operand if the destination is larger than or equal to the source operand.
JB JNAE JC	I	Chapter 10	JUMP IF BELOW Transfers control to the target operand if the destination is smaller than the source operand.
JBE JNA	I		JUMP IF BELOW OR EQUAL Transfers control to the target operand if the destination is smaller than or equal to the source operand.

(continued)

INSTRUCTIONS AND DIRECTIVES (coninued)

NAME	I OR D	REFERENCE CHAPTER	DESCRIPTION
JC JB JNAE	I	Chapter 7	JUMP ON CARRY Transfers control to the target operand if the carry flag is set.
JE JZ	I	Chapter 5 Chapter 4	JUMP ON EQUAL OR ZERO Transfers control to the target operand if the destination and the source operands are equal (zero flag is set).
JMP	I	Chapter 3	JUMP (unconditional) Transfers control to the target label unconditionally.
JNC JAE JNB	I	Chapter 6	JUMP IF NO CARRY Transfers control to the target operand if the carry flag is clear.
JNE JNZ	I	Chapter 4 Chapter 3	JUMP IF NOT EQUAL OR NOT ZERO Transfers control to the target operand if the destination and source operands are not equal.
LEA	I	Chapter 2	LOAD EFFECTIVE ADDRESS Transfers the offset of a memory operand to the destination operand, which must be a 16-bit general register.
LOOP	I	Chapter 3	LOOP Decrements the CX register and transfers control to the target if CX is not 0. If CX = 0 execution drops to the next instruction.
MOV	I	Chapter 2	MOVE (byte or word) Transfers a byte or word from the source to the destination operand.
MUL	I	Chapter 7	MULTIPLY Unsigned multiplication of the source operand and the accumulator. The operation can take the forms: AL * byte source = product in AX AX * word source = product in DX:AX When the CF and OF are set, AH or DX contain significant digits.
NOT	I	Chapter 4	LOGICAL NOT Performs a logical NOT operation of two byte- or word-size operands. The NOT operation forms the 1's complement of a number by inverting all bits.
OR	I	Chapter 4	LOGICAL OR Inclusive OR of a byte or word operand. A bit in the result is set if either or both operand bits are set Otherwise the bit is cleared.

(continued)

INSTRUCTIONS AND DIRECTIVES (coninued)

NAME	I OR D	REFERENCE CHAPTER	DESCRIPTION
OUT	I		OUTPUT (byte or word) Transfers a byte or word form the AL or AX register to a designated output port. The port number can be specified as an operand or entered in the DX register. The latter form allows access to port numbers up to 65,535.
POP	I	Chapter 3	POP STACK Transfers the word at the top of the stack to a memory, register, or segment register operand and increments the SP by two to point to a new stack top. POP CS is not allowed.
PROC	D	Chapter 3	PROCEDURE DEFINITION Directive to assign a name (symbol) to a procedure and define its distance. NEAR procedures must be located in the same segment as the CALL instruction. FAR procedures are located in another segment. The type of RET instruction (near or far) is selected by the assembler according to how the procedure was defined (NEAR or FAR).
PUSH	I	Chapter 3	PUSH The stack top pointer is decremented by two and the word operand is transferred to the location pointed by SP. The PUSH and POP sequence is used to store data on the stack and for passing parameters to a procedure.
RET	I	Chapter 3	RETURN FROM PROCEDURE Transfers control to the instruction following the CALL.
SAL SHL	I	Chapter 3	SHIFT ARITHMETIC LEFT All bits in the byte or word operand are shifted left. In 8086-88 systems the shift count must be 1 or the value stored in CL.
SAR	I		SHIFT ARITHMETIC RIGHT Bits in the byte or word operand are shifted right. The shift count must be 1 or the value stored in CL.
STC	I	Chapter 6	SET CARRY FLAG Set the carry flag (CF = 1). This instruction can be used to pass a return code to an error handler.
STI	I	Chapter 8	SET INTERRUPT FLAG Sets the interrupt-enable flag making the processor recognize maskable interrupt requests on the INTR line.

(continued)

INSTRUCTIONS AND DIRECTIVES (coninued)

NAME	I OR D	REFERENCE CHAPTER	D E S C R I P T I O N
SUB	I	Chapter 3	SUBTRACT Subract the source operand from the destination. The operands may be bytes or words and signed or unsigned binary numbers.
TEST	I	Chapter 3	TEST Updates the flags as if a logical AND operation of the two operands had been performed. If the TEST operation is followed by a JNZ instruction, the jump will be taken if there are corresponding one-bits in both operands.
XOR	I	Chapter 4	EXCLUSIVE OR Performs the EXCLUSIVE OR of a byte or word operand and returns the result to the destination operand. A bit in the result is set if the corresponding bits in both operands contain opposite values.

Appendix D - IBM Character Set

Characters ØH to 7FH								
Hex	Ø	1	2	3	4	5	6	7
Ø		►		Ø	@	P	`	p
1	☺	◄	!	1	A	Q	a	q
2	●	↕	"	2	B	R	b	r
3	♥	‼	#	3	C	S	c	s
4	♦	¶	$	4	D	T	d	t
5	♣	§	%	5	E	U	e	u
6	♠	▬	&	6	F	V	f	v
7	•	↨	'	7	G	W	g	w
8	◘	↑	(	8	H	X	h	x
9	○	↓	)	9	I	Y	i	y
A	◎	→	*	:	J	Z	j	z
B	♂	←	+	;	K	[	k	{
C	♀	∟	,	<	L	\	l	¦
D	♪	↔	-	=	M	]	m	}
E	♫	▲	.	>	N	^	n	~
F	☼	▼	/	?	O	_	o	Δ

(continued)

Characters 7FH to FFH							
Hex	**8**	**9**	**A**	**B**	**C**	**D**	**E**	**F**
0	Ç	É	á	░	└	╨	α	≡
1	ü	æ	í	▒	┴	╤	β	±
2	é	Æ	ó	▓	┬	╥	Γ	≥
3	â	ô	ú	│	├	╙	π	≤
4	ä	ö	ñ	┤	─	╘	Σ	⌠
5	à	ò	Ñ	╡	┼	╒	σ	⌡
6	å	û	ª	╢	╞	╓	μ	÷
7	ç	ù	º	╖	╟	╫	τ	≈
8	ê	ÿ	¿	╕	╚	╪	Φ	○
9	ë	Ö	⌐	╣	╔	┘	Θ	•
A	è	Ü	¬	║	╩	┌	Ω	·
B	ï	¢	½	╗	╦	█	δ	√
C	î	£	¼	╝	╠	▄	∞	ⁿ
D	ì	¥	¡	╜	=	█	φ	²
E	Ä	₧	«	╛	╬	█	∈	■
F	Å	ƒ	»	┐	┴	▄	∩	

Bibliography

ANGERMEYER, JOHN, AND KEVIN JAEGER. *MS DOS Developer's Guide*. Indianapolis, IN: Howard W. Sams, 1986.

BRADLEY, DAVID J. *Assembly Language Programming for the IBM Personal Computer*. Englewood Cliffs, NJ: Prentice Hall, 1984.

CHIEN, CHAO C. *Programming the IBM Personal Computer: Assembly Language*. New York: CBS College Publishing.

DAVIS, WILLIAM S. *Computing Fundamentals - Concepts*. 2nd ed. Reading, MA: Addison-Wesley, 1989.

DUNCAN, RAY. *Advanced MS DOS*. Redmond, WA: Microsoft Press, 1986.

FRANKLIN, MARK. *Using the IBM PC: Organization and Assembly Language Programming*. New York: CBS College Publishing.

GOFTON, PETER W. *Mastering Serial Communications*. San Francisco: Sybex, 1986

HOGAN, THOM. *The Programmer's PC Sourcebook*. Redmond, WA: Microsoft Press, 1988.

IBM CORPORATION. *Personal System/2 and Personal Computer BIOS Interface Technical Reference*. Boca Raton, FL: IBM, 1987.

———. *Technical Reference, Personal Computer*. Boca Raton, FL: IBM, 1984.

INTEL CORPORATION. *iAPX 86/88, 186/188 User's Manual* (Programmer's Reference). Santa Clara, CA: Reward Books, 1983.

———. *iAPX 86/88, 186/188 User's Manual* (Programmer's Reference). Santa Clara, CA: Intel, 1987.

JOURDAIN, ROBERT. *Programmer's Problem Solver for the IBM PC, XT & AT*. New York: Brady Communications, 1986.

JUMP, DENNIS N. *Programmer's Guide to MS DOS for the IBM PC*. Reston, VA: Brady Communications, 1984.

LIU, YU-CHENG AND GLENN A. GIBSON. *Microcomputer Systems: The 8086/8088 Family*. Englewood Cliffs, NJ: Prentice Hall, 1984.

MORGAN, CHRISTOPHER L. *Bluebook of Assembly Language Routines for the IBM PC & XT*. New York: Waite Group, 1984.

NORTON, PETER. *Inside the IBM PC* (Access to Advanced Features and Programming). Bowie, MD: Robert J. Brady Co., 1983.

———. *Peter Norton's Assembly Language Book for the IBM PC*. New York: Brady Communications, 1986.

———. *The Peter Norton Programmer's Guide to the IBM PC*. Redmond, WA: Microsoft Press, 1985.

RALSTON, ANTHONY, AND CHESTER L. MEEK. *Encyclopedia of Computer Science*. New York: Mason and Charter, 1983.

ROYER, JEFFREY P. *Handbook of Software & Hardware Interfacing for the IBM PCs*. Englewood Cliffs, NJ: Prentice Hall, 1987.

SANCHEZ, JULIO. *Assembly Language Tools and Techniques for the IBM Microcomputers*. Englewood Cliffs, NJ: Prentice Hall, 1990.

———. Graphics Design and Animation on the IBM Microcomputers. Englewood Cliffs, NJ: Prentice Hall, 1990.

SANCHEZ, JULIO, AND MARIA P. CANTON. *IBM Microcomputers: A Programmer's Handbook*. New York: McGraw-Hill, 1990.

———. *Programming Solutions Handbook for the IBM Microcomputers*. New York: McGraw-Hill, 1991.

SARGENT, RICHARD, III, AND RICHARD L. SHOEMAKER. *The IBM Personal Computer from the Inside Out*. Reading, MA: Addison-Wesley, 1984.

SCANLON, LEO J. *Assembly Language Subroutines for MS-DOS Computers*. Blue Ridge Summit, PA: Tab Professional and Reference Books, 1987.

———. *IBM PC & XT Assembly Language*. Bowie, MD: Brady Communications, 1983.

SCHATT, STAN. *Understanding Local Area Networks*. Indianapolis, IN: Howard W. Sams, 1987.

SEYER, MARTIN D. *RS-232 Made Easy*. Englewood Cliffs, NJ: Prentice Hall, 1984.

SMITH, BUD E., AND MARK T. JOHNSON. *Programming the Intel 80386*. Glenview, IL: Scott, Foresman Computer Books, 1987.

SMITH, JAMES T. *The IBM PC AT Programmer' Guide*. New York: Waite Group, 1986.

STALLINGS, WILLIAM. *Handbook of Computer Communications Standards*. Volumes 1-3. New York: Macmillan, 1988.

STARTS, RICHARD. *8087 Applications and Programming for the IBM PC, XT, and AT*. New York: Brady Communications, 1985.

WILLEN, DAVID C. *IBM PCjr Assembler Language*. Indianapolis, IN: Howard W. Sams, 1984.

WILLEN, DAVID C., AND JEFFREY I. KRANTZ. *8088 Assembler Language Programming: The IBM PC*. Indianapolis, IN: Howard W. Sams, 1983.

WORAM, JOHN. *The PC Configuration Handbook*. New York: Bantam Books, 1987.

Index

Prentice Hall
Englewood Cliffs, New Jersey
07632

The Prentice Hall Programming Skills Series

MS-DOS SURVIVAL KIT

1. Starting the System

Before you turn on a computer equipped with a hard disk drive make sure that the diskette drive is empty. This does not apply if you wish to boot using an MS-DOS diskette. Most computers are turned on from a power strip or a master switch. In this case, the machine's individual switches (system unit, monitor, printer, etc.) should be on. If the switches on the individual components are on, the power strip is connected to the power supply, and the machine still does not respond, get help from the instructor or the lab assistant. DO NOT TINKER.

(Fold)

To copy files from the current drive and directory you may omit this parameter. For example, if you are logged on to drive A you may type:

COPY *.* C:\QUICKB < Enter >

10. Copying a Diskette or Microdisk

The MS-DOS DISKCOPY command is used to re-produce an entire diskette or microdisk for backup or other purposes. DISKCOPY automatically formats the destination media if it has not been previously fomatted or if the format is not compatible with the source. DISKCOPY cannot be used to copy groups of files. Use the COPY command and a global filename instead. To copy a microdisk or diskette in a single drive system type the command:

DISKCOPY A: B: < Enter >

In order to preform this operation MS-DOS creates a virtual drive B.

TITLES IN THE PRENTICE HALL
PROGRAMMING SKILLS SERIES

IBM® Microcomputer Assembly Language
in 10 Programming Lessons

C Language in 10 Programming Lessons

Pascal in 10 Programming Lessons

BASIC in 10 Programming Lessons

COBOL in 10 Programming Lessons

(Fold)

IBM DISKETTE FORMATS

Capacity	Type	System
360K	5 1/4-in DD	PC, PC XT, and compatible
1200K	5 1/4-in QD	PC AT, HP Vectra, and compatible
720K	3 1/2-in DD	PS/2 Model 25 and Model 30
1440K	3 1/2-in HD	PS/2 Model 30-386, 50, 60, 70, 80, 90, and compatible

To format a diskette or micro disk in drive A to the system's standard capacity type the command:

FORMAT A: < Enter >

To format a 360K diskette on a 1200K drive (AT or HP Vectra) type:

FORMAT A:/4 < Enter >

To format a 720K microdisk on a 1440K drive type the command:

FORMAT A:/N:9/T:80 < Enter >

To create a diskette or microdisk with the MS-DOS files required to start-up the system (system disk) use the /S option of the FORMAT command, as follows:

FORMAT A: /S < Enter >

9. Copying Files

The MS-DOS COPY command is used to copy one or more files. The MS-DOS wildcard characters ? and * can be used with the copy command. For example, to copy all files from the root directory in drive A to the directory \QUICKB in drive C, type the command:

COPY A:*.* C:\QUICKB < Enter >

2. Drives and Directories

In the IBM microcomputer information is stored on magnetic diskettes or in a fixed disk. All IBM microcomputers have at least one disk or diskette drive. Most systems have two drives: a diskette drive and a fixed disk. The diskette drives are normally designated with the letters A and B. The fixed disk will normally appear as drive C, although it can be partitioned into more than one logical drive (D, E, F, and so on). Drives are designated by the drive letter followed by a colon, for example:

A:

Data stored in magnetic media is classified in directories and subdirectories. Every diskette or fixed disk drive contains a root directory, identified by the \ symbol. Directory and subdirectory names can have up to eight letters, numbers, and special symbols. The following special symbols are allowed in file and directory names:) , (# _ &

3. The Pathname

The pathname is the location of a file in the system's drive and directory structure. The pathname can contain a drive letter, one or more directories and subdirectories, and a filename. The following is an example of a pathname:

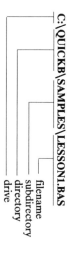

C:\QUICKB\SAMPLES\LESSON1.BAS

- filename
- subdirectory
- directory
- drive

Not all pathnames have all of these elements. The following pathname contains only the drive and a filename:

A:\TEMPLATE.ASM

To *log on* to a drive, type the drive letter followed by the colon symbol and press the <Enter> key. To log-on to a directory or subdirectory type the command CD (change directory) followed by a backslash, then the pathname, for example:

COMMAND	ACTION
C: <Enter>	log-on to drive C
CD\QB<Enter>	log-on to directory QB

4. MS-DOS Files and Filenames

An MS-DOS document or program is stored as a magnetic record called a file. MS-DOS files are identified by an eight character filename and an optional three character extension. The filename is separated by a period from the extension. Filenames can contain letters, numbers, and the special characters) , (# _ &. The following are MS-DOS filenames:

MYFILE_1.PRG
LEDC.EXE

while the filename LESSON1.* represents the files:

LESSON1.BAS
LESSON1.EXE
LESSON1.MAP

The expression *.* applies to all files, whatever their filename or extension.

The * symbol is used to represent several unspecified characters in the filename or the extension fields. For example, the filename WP*.* represents the following files:

WP.EXE
WPDEMO.FIL
WPLISTA.DOC

5. The Directory Tree

The structure of directories and subdirectories in a diskette, microdisk, or fixed disk is called the directorytree. If no directories exist then the directorytree is simply the root directory. The MS-DOS TREE command displays the directory tree in the active drive. The following is a directory tree:

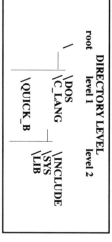

DIRECTORY LEVEL		
root	level 1	level 2
\	\DOS	
	\C_LANG	\INCLUDE
		\SYS
		\LIB
	\QUICK_B	

6. MS-DOS Wildcard Characters

MS-DOS allows the use of placeholder characters in filenames. The ? symbol is a placeholder for any unspecified character. For example, the filename: LESSON?.BAS represents the following files:

LESSON1.BAS
LESSON2.BAS
LESSONA.BAS

7. MS-DOS DIR Command

MS-DOS stores and maintains a list of all the files in each directory and subdirectory. Various forms of the MS-DOS DIR command can be used to see the list of the files and directories in a drive or the files and subdirectories in a directory. For example:

COMMAND	ACTION
DIR <Enter>	Lists files in current drive, directory, or subdirectory
DIR A: <Enter>	Lists files in drive A
DIR /P<Enter>	Lists files and pauses after each full screen
DIR /W <Enter>	Lists files in compressed form
DIR \QB<Enter>	Lists files in directory \QB
DIR *.ASM<Enter>	Lists all files with extension .ASM
DIR *.<Enter>	Lists all files with no extension (can be used to list subdirectories)

8. Formatting

The MS-DOS FORMAT command checks a fixed disk, diskette, or microdisk for defects and creates a magnetic pattern of concentric circles that is necessary for storing data. WARNING: the FORMAT command erases all previously recorded data.